W9-ACX-761

WAYNE PUBLIC LIBRARY WAYNE N.J

NOV 1 7 1997

TRUMP'S TOP TEN COMEBACK TIPS

1. PLAY GOLF

It helped me relax and concentrate. It took my mind off my problems; I only thought about putting the ball in the hole. And, the irony is, I made lots of money on the golf course—making contacts and deals and coming up with ideas.

2. STAY FOCUSED

I am convinced that if I had maintained the same work ethic I had during the 1970s and most of the 1980s, there would have been no recession for me. I wasn't focused and really thought that life and success just came hand in hand. I thought I was better than the rest. When I began to relax and take it a little—or perhaps a lot—easier things began to fall apart.

3. BE PARANOID

I have noticed over the years that people who are guarded or, to put it more coldly, slightly paranoid, end up being the most successful. Let some paranoia reign! You've got to realize that you have something other people want. Don't let them take it away.

4. BE PASSIONATE

This is a key ingredient to success and to coming back. If you don't have passion about who you are, about what you are trying to be, about where you are going, you might as well close this book right now and give up. Go get a job and relax, because you have no chance of making it. Passion is the essence of life and certainly the essence of success.

5. GO AGAINST THE TIDE

When I decided to keep 40 Wall Street as an office building, everyone in lower Manhattan was converting their buildings to residential space—and with good reason. The apartment market is hot as a pistol. I decided to head in the exact opposite direction, and now I am signing up tenants at rents far higher than anything I expected.

6. GO WITH YOUR GUT

Some of the greatest investors I have ever known invest by instinct, rather than research, study, or hard work. If you look back over history, this is the way the greatest fortunes have been built. People had ideas that they truly believed in.

7. WORK WITH PEOPLE YOU LIKE

If you go to the office and don't find the energy in the people you are with, it is highly unlikely that you will be energized toward success.

8. BE LUCKY

I hate to put this in the book because it can't be acquired. People who inherit fortunes are lucky; I call them members of the lucky sperm club. But you can help coax luck into your life by working hard and being at the right place at the right time.

9. GET EVEN

During the bad times, I learned who was loyal and who wasn't. I believe in an eye for an eye. A couple of people who betrayed me need my help now, and I am screwing them against the wall! I am doing a number . . . and I'm having so much fun.

10. ALWAYS HAVE A PRENUPTIAL AGREEMENT

Anyone in a complicated business should be institutionalized if he or she gets married without one. I know firsthand that you can't come back if you're spending all of your time fighting for your financial life with a spouse.

TRUMP

THE ART OF THE COMEBACK

ALSO BY DONALD TRUMP

Trump: The Art of the Deal

Trump: Surviving at the Top

TRUMP

THE ART OF THE COMEBACK

Donald J. Trump
with Kate Bohner

TIMES 𝕿 BOOKS

RANDOM HOUSE

Copyright © 1997 by Donald Trump
All rights reserved under International and Pan-American Copyright
Conventions. Published in the United States by Times Books, a
division of Random House, Inc., New York, and simultaneously in
Canada by Random House of Canada Limited, Toronto.

*Grateful acknowledgment is made to the following for permission to
reprint previously published material:*

The New York Times: Excerpt from a restaurant review of Jean
Georges by Ruth Reichl (June 6, 1997). Copyright © 1997 by The
New York Times Co. Reprinted by permission.

All photos not otherwise credited courtesy the Trump collection.

Library of Congress Cataloging-in-Publication Data

Trump, Donald J.
Trump : the art of the comeback / Donald Trump with Kate Bohner.
        p.   cm.
Includes index.
ISBN 0-8129-2964-0 (alk. paper)
1. Trump, Donald.   2. Businessmen—United States—Biography.
3. Real estate developers—United States—Biography.   I. Bohner,
Kate.   II. Title.
HC102.5.T78A3   1997
333.33'092—dc21
[B]   97-37296

Random House website address: http://www.randomhouse.com/
Printed in the United States of America on acid-free paper
24689753
First Edition
BOOK DESIGN BY HELENE BERINSKY

For my parents, Fred and Mary,
my brothers, Robert and the late Fred Jr.,
and my sisters, Maryanne and Elizabeth

You can't make an omelette without breaking eggs.
—*Robert Moses*

Victory at all costs, victory in spite of all terror, victory however long and hard the road may be; for without victory there is no survival.
—*Winston Churchill*

The physician can bury his mistakes, but the architect can only advise his client to plant vines.
—*Frank Lloyd Wright*

CONTENTS

CONTENTS

Coming back means it never stops—even at a U.S. Open tennis match.

INTRODUCTION

It's usually fun being The Donald, but in the early 1990s, trust me, it wasn't. My journey is a hard one to believe. I was many billions in the red, $975 million of that debt I'd personally guaranteed. The banks were crawling all over me. The Gulf War had a disastrous effect on tourism. Cash flows were dwindling at my casinos. Then I missed a mortgage payment on the Castle in Atlantic City. All hell broke loose. Wall Street went nuts. The newspapers screamed of my demise. I was up against the wall. So I sold a few assets to stay afloat. Then, after being pummeled by my bankers, Ivana turned around and sued me for $2 billion. Life, I thought, looked bleak.

Then, one day around Christmas of 1990 I said to myself, Donald, it's time to fight back. So I got down to work. Today I'm over $3 billion in the black, I've paid off my personal debt, business is great, I'm single (and available!), and I'm loving life.

I'm a firm believer in learning from adversity. Often the worst of times can turn to your advantage—my life is a study of that. I learned so much during the tough years. So I decided to write it all down. If you're in trouble, or you're down and out, I hope you'll be able to glean some of my hard-learned lessons in these pages. This isn't just a book about the ins and outs of deal making—how to make deals come about, how to get the goods and close the deal. My wish is that this book will provide inspiration. It's a tale that almost anyone, whether a broker, trader, lawyer, real estate exec, publisher, even a homemaker (something I know nothing about), can learn from.

I learned a lot about myself during these hard times; I learned about handling pressure. I was able to home in, buckle down, get back to the basics, and make things work. I worked much harder, I focused, and I got myself out of a box. Don't get me wrong—there were moments of doubt, but I never thought in negative terms. I believe in positive thought and positive thinking.

I learned a lot about loyalty—who was and who wasn't. There were people that I would have guaranteed would have stuck by me who didn't, and, on the other hand, people who I had *made* who, when it came time to help me, didn't lift a finger.

Take Sam LeFrak. He's crude by any standard, and I've always said that he is the least respected successful man I have ever met. Sam has a wonderful family, and his son, Richard, is truly outstanding. When I watch Richard in action, it's hard to believe that Sam could have produced such a guy. In any event, like all else having to do with loyalty, Sam LeFrak will kiss my ass in person. People would tell me he was saying rotten things about me. I have no idea whether he did or not. Whenever I asked him, he would deny it. "Donny, I never fuckin' said that," he would proclaim when, in fact, I never had any doubts that he did. When times were good, Sam was very nice to me. I was told that as soon as things started getting bad, he was openly happy, not to my face but behind my back.

Now Sam is calling all the time asking for anything, breakfast, lunch, dinner—just any kind of association. I sent him a copy of an article in which he slyly derided me. On top of the article I wrote just two words: "Fuck you."

As a result of these experiences, my thinking has changed. I'm sharper. I'm warier. I believe in an eye for an eye—like the Old Testament says. Some of the people who forgot to lift a finger when I needed them, when I was down, they need *my* help now, and I'm screwing them against the wall. I'm doing a number . . . and I'm having so much fun. People say that's not nice, but I really believe in getting even.

On the other hand, there were those I wouldn't have completely counted on who were loyal to the nth degree. These people were not only loyal, they were warriors. They supported me and saw me through—these are the people I have learned to rely on.

What I love is doing deals. I also enjoy writing. My first book, *Trump: The Art of the Deal,* became an immediate *New York Times* number-one best-seller and was a terrific experience. Judging from the letters I received, and the "buzz" the book generated, I reached a lot more people than I thought I would. In this book I hope to do the same. My second book, *Trump: Surviving at the Top,* was also a number-one *Times* best-seller, despite the fact that my heart was never in it. Now I am doing the book that I wanted to do even more than my first book.

Another thing I'd like to do in this book—in fact, right now—is to apologize to two men I was too tough on in my last book.

Malcolm Forbes is perhaps the best business editor of the twentieth century, and I wish I had given him greater respect in print. At the

YUKON ARCHIVES/ATLIN HISTORICAL SOCIETY COLLECTION

The First Trump Frontier: My grandfather came all the way from Germany to Alaska and owned a small piece of this strip in the Yukon—it must be in the genes.

My father, Robert, and me: Three very different kinds of guys.

RON GALELLA (NOT TO BE REPRODUCED WITHOUT PERMISSION)

*The apple of my eye: My stunning, sweet daughter
Ivanka.*

time I was writing *Trump: Surviving at the Top*, *Forbes* magazine was attacking me unmercifully and, I thought, unfairly. In looking back over the last couple of years, since Malcolm's death, I realize that New York City lost a true character in him, a great asset, someone who added a lot of spice and excitement to a very complex and often forbidding city. Not many people are able to be heard in New York—but Malcolm was, and I see now, much more than I did two years ago, how much he is missed and even needed. Besides, why the hell should I be attacking him if his magazine goes after me? Malcolm was gone, he wasn't the one kicking my ass, and maybe he might not have liked seeing me beat up because I have this strange symbiotic relationship

ANGELIKA RINNHOFER

Now a poised and elegant young lady, Ivanka stands on the brink of a successful modeling career. I couldn't be more proud.

with New York, a city that Malcolm truly loved. When I'm attacked, in a strange way, so is New York. In any event, I realize now, much more than at the time of his death, that Malcolm Forbes brought great vitality and wisdom to a place that can use all the vitality and wisdom it can get.

Another one of my biggest regrets about my second book was how harshly I wrote about Frank Sinatra. I didn't mean it to come out the way it did. It was a strange evening, the night I met him. I reported about how Sinatra, over dinner in Monte Carlo with Ivana and me and another couple, blew up at his wife, Barbara, and made some fairly rude comments about women in general. I was shocked at

Me and my cousins from Brooklyn. (Okay, only kidding. Just wanted to make sure you were paying attention.)

Malcolm Forbes was a dynamic businessman and New York misses him.

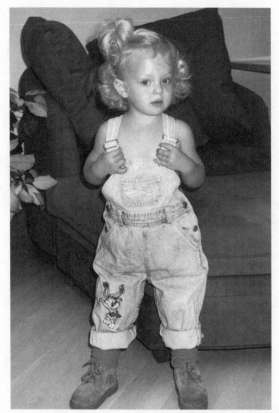

Tiffany Trump: The little girl who makes me laugh.

the time, but what I realize now is, hey, the guy has got a hell of a lot of pressure on him. He can't walk through a lobby without a hundred people asking for his autograph. I didn't take this into account. Dealing with fame can truly be a hassle. Believe me, Frank, I realize that now. I shouldn't have written the things that I did, and I'm sorry.

I've come to realize that the entertainment business is the most vicious industry of all, probably the hardest place to maintain a top position. Younger and better-looking talents are waiting by the thousands to push you off the perch. Frank Sinatra has not only survived for six decades, since he was a teenager, but he is, as everybody in the industry knows, "the Chairman of the Board." While I haven't spoken to Frank since my last book was published, and I don't necessarily intend to speak to him again, I want to set the record straight. Perhaps he is different, perhaps he is tough, and perhaps he can even be nasty at times, but he has done one hell of a job, and there are very few like him.

I believe that in order to succeed, or get to a place where you can start thinking about the future, you really have to focus on the present. My policy is to learn from the past, focus on the present, and dream about the future. The danger in dreaming too much is that there are so many things beyond our control—wars, famine, anything

Hillary Clinton, Donny Jr., Eric, and me. The First Lady is a wonderful woman who has handled pressure incredibly well.

SARAH MERIANS PHOTOGRAPHY

can happen. At least with the present you can factor in what's going on now; you have some control. But the future? The future is very tough to predict.

So I stay in the present and concentrate on current events. Luckily, I do every deal because I enjoy it. I don't do it for the money—the money just seems to flow in. People don't believe that—they laugh when I say it because they think I'm totally money-oriented. I'm not.

So, it's been a terrific period of time, an amazing period of time. It's good to come out of a rough time because you really appreciate what you have much more. In the eighties it seemed so simple, whereas now I look at every deal I've done and appreciate the work and energy I've put into it. I enjoy my successes much more because I realize it wasn't so easy after all.

TRUMP

THE ART OF THE COMEBACK

Believe it or not, I think I've made more money on the golf course than Jack Nicklaus.

THE BATTLE BEGINS:

BARGAINING WITH THE BANKS

IT NEVER OCCURRED TO ME TO GIVE UP, TO ADMIT DEFEAT. True, I was billions of dollars in the hole. The real estate market had disintegrated. Bodies were dropping right and left. Banks folded. The junk-bond market was collapsing. There was no end in sight to the bad news.

Front-page headlines heralded my downfall. I became the poster boy for the recession. Friends and family called to offer condolences and support. Oddly enough, I wasn't that miserable. Sure, the chips were down. There were some dark moments. But I never had any doubt that I'd come back.

I will never forget what happened on March 26, 1991. Both *The New York Times* and *The Wall Street Journal* had front-page stories predicting my demise, detailing the financial trouble I was in. Anybody with a brain who read those stories would have said I was finished. The stories were picked up by radio and television and blasted throughout the world. This was by far the worst moment of my life.

I was in my office, and there was dead silence. The phone had stopped ringing because even my closest friends felt it would be better to stay away from me rather than call in their regrets—something I always hated anyway. It was then that Rhona Graff, my very loyal secretary, came into my office and told me that Ivana was on the phone. We were separated at the time, and I thought to myself, how nice, Ivana was calling with her sympathies or, even better, with encouragement. That really was sweet! As it turned out, that was not at all the purpose of Ivana's phone call. I picked up the phone and said, "Hello, Ivana, how are you?" Ivana said, as cold as ice, "I vant my money now. I vant my money now. I have decided to honor the contract, and I vant a check for ten million dollars and all the other things immediately. I am no longer going to court. I vant my money now."

Then she hung up, and I said to myself, "Wow, what a mess!"

At that moment I realized it was time to go back to work. I had taken a siesta. I had relied on other people, many of them "highly trained and educated executives." Sure, success in business takes education and training. But it all comes down to feel and touch. I've got the instincts. That's how I'd gotten on top in the first place. I wasn't using my instincts anymore. I'd gotten bored, taken my eye off the ball. Why, I thought, should I work my ass off when I can get somebody to do it for me? Everything had gotten too easy. My life had been a series of wins with few, if any, failures. I went to the great

Wharton School of Finance and did well. I'd quickly built a huge and successful company. I'd made few mistakes, certainly none I could remember as having great consequence.

I'll always remember that day in 1980, standing at the corner of Fifth Avenue and Fifty-seventh Street, watching Trump Tower begin to rise. Even before the construction started, I was selling apartments at a rate that few people had witnessed before. While I was looking up, someone tapped me on the shoulder and said, "Hi, Donald, how are you doing?" I looked over, and it was Jerry Speyer, head of the Tishman Realty firm. He's a development pro. Jerry's a little older than me and, as it turns out, at that time at least, a little wiser.

I began to tell him what a great success I was having renting the retail space and selling the apartments in Trump Tower. The atrium, I said, was a spectacular success. He had heard that and congratulated me. Then he paused and said, in effect, "Be careful of the markets because when the markets change you could take the best apartment in any building in New York City and it's got virtually no sale value." I listened to him but sort of laughed to myself. That was impossible, I thought. Look at the way things were going. Even in a bad market I'd be able to sell apartments at Fifth Avenue and Fifty-seventh Street!

I got a little cocky and, probably, a little bit lazy. I wasn't working as hard, and I wasn't focusing on the basics. I traveled around the world to the spring fashion shows in France. What the hell did I have to travel to Paris for when we have better fashion shows in New York? The models were the same. Believe me, the clothes were beautiful, but I wasn't looking at the clothes.

I began to socialize more, probably too much. Frankly, I was bored. I really felt I could do no wrong. Sort of like a baseball player who keeps hitting home runs or a golfer who keeps winning tournaments—you just get a feeling of invincibility. Ultimately, this invincible feeling, while positive at times, can be destructive. You let down your guard. You don't work as hard. Then things start to go in the wrong direction. And that's what happened to me—and I never thought it could. Sadly, Jerry was right that day on Fifth Avenue. Eleven years later, in 1990, the market was so horrendous that prices, for even the best buildings in town, were plummeting. Apartments were being bought at prices you never thought possible. It was a complete disaster.

I personally witnessed the end of the real estate market and the beginning of what I term the Great Depression of 1990. That's right: I use the word *depression.* It was not a recession. It was, in fact, a depression, more severe than anything that had taken place since the early 1930s. Real estate markets were reeling. Banks were failing. Certain industries—retailing, the airlines, and countless others—were being virtually wiped out. You had to be really good to survive. And, sadly, you had to be lucky. Many of my friends were talented but not talented enough. Those friends are gone—never to be seen again on the business front. Many filed for bankruptcy, and many just gave up. They cashed in their chips or, far worse than that, were forced to work for someone else—pretty tough when you have always worked for yourself.

Take my good friend, a real estate executive who had built up a fairly good fortune. Before writing this, I asked if it would be possible for me to say something about him. "Absolutely, Donald," he said. "But please don't use my name. I'm starting my new life, and it's beginning to work out okay." This guy had a number of successful buildings and was well on his way to "going to the top." In 1989 he was worth at least $50 million. He's a terrific guy, but he believed in laying all his chips down at once. It turned out his timing was wrong. By the end of 1990 he was completely wiped out. His wife and family had left him, and he started to drink heavily. It was a very sad day when he came into my office and asked me to help him get a job. I was certainly having my own problems at the time. But he had no money and, in fact, was overqualified for any kind of a job available to him. Because he had helped me in the mid-1970s, when I was just starting out, I made a concerted effort to help him. It paid off. Today he is a successful executive within another company. But he will never be able to attain the success he once had. He refers to those times as just a chapter in his life.

Another good friend of mine, a very successful guy in the seventies and eighties, built a fortune of about $500 million, mostly in real estate. He had four children whom he loved very much and decided, in 1988, to give each child $10 million. He made this gift without hesitation and not knowing that shortly thereafter a very bad time would be upon us. In 1990 and 1991 he was experiencing tremendous financial difficulty. He decided to go back to his children, to whom he had given this gift of $40 million, and ask each for $7.5 million so he could pay off bank loans at substantial discounts. It was a great opportunity for him, and he never had a doubt that they would gladly give him the money. He called a meeting, and to his amazement the kids were dead set against returning even the smallest amount. They said to him, "Look, Dad, you got yourself into trouble. That's not our fault. You shouldn't ask us to give back the money you gave us."

He walked out of that room in total disbelief. I saw this man recently, and his business is again doing well. He was able to survive without the help of his kids. When I said to him, "How are your children? Have you ever forgiven them?"

He said, "Donald, what children are you talking about? I have no children, they're dead."

I think this is a very sad story and truly feel that his children should be totally ashamed of themselves.

In contrast, my father and I are very close—he really helped me through the bad times. Fred Trump is a rough-and-tumble guy and a wonderful businessman. He has always taken great pride in my success and for fifteen years he has backed me wherever possible, never wavering once. Well, when times got bad, he continued to stand by me. He had no doubt that I would make it back. He would tell people, "Don't worry about Donald, I've watched him all of his life. Donald is a winner and will have no trouble. Times are tough for everyone, but Donald will be the one who ends up on top." I have always appreciated his confidence in me.

Another horrifying story, again the opposite of my own experience, involves a man I know who made a large bequest to a well-known university. The bequest was to be paid over a long period, but the amounts of money were substantial. When this man got into trouble in the early 1990s, he went to the university to ask its indulgence and essentially seek a temporary reduction or cessation of payment. He left the meeting feeling really good and believing his was a routine request that would be honored. Unfortunately, the following week he was delivered a legal notice demanding payment in full and stipulating that if the payment was not made, the university would immediately start a court action seeking the money and damages based on his pledge.

He told me that never again would he get involved in such a situation, and as he makes his final payment to the school next year, he will be happy in the knowledge that he will never have to make another payment to that institution. He is a very rich man again, and had this school behaved properly, the money it could have ultimately received would have been far greater than what he had already given. Because of this, whenever I make a long-term commitment to a school or charity, I stipulate that I have the right, at any time and for any reason, to stop payment. Times change, economies change, and the world changes—and I won't be caught.

My blip—as I call my difficult time—was much different from that of my friends. It was more a sabbatical of sorts. If I'd had my eye on the ball, I'm sure I would have seen more of the problems on the economic horizon. The truth is, I did see some. I got nervous when

Washington passed a ludicrous tax law in 1986—it ended up being a disaster for both real estate and banking and caused the depression of 1990–1993. More on that later.

The fact is, I saw the signs. So I started selling. Unfortunately, when I want to sell, nobody else wants to buy because they figure I know something more than they do. Why should they buy something Donald Trump doesn't want?

Fortunately, I did get off one deal before the deluge—and it was a beauty. I had acquired a terrific property in midtown Manhattan for $70 million from Harry and Leona Helmsley, and a short while later, in 1989, I sold it to Alan Bond for $180 million. That's about a $110 million profit on the deal, which just reinforced what I stated before, that I felt I could do no wrong, that I didn't know how to hit anything less than a grand slam home run. Here I'd bought a building from the great Harry Helmsley (and he was indeed a great man who, unfortunately, married the wrong woman) and sold it at a huge profit. In my eyes this further proved my invincibility. How could I possibly fail? I'd had incredible success with the Grand Hyatt Hotel; cash poured in from my casinos in Atlantic City; Trump Tower condos stayed on the market for about a minute. It was a fantastic time, like the Roaring Twenties. But of course, it couldn't last. I learned at the Wharton School of Finance that the economy runs in cycles. I guess I forgot the second half of the lesson, along with everyone else in business: Eventually, something's got to give.

This time, the give was precipitated by the U.S. government, more specifically, by Congress. It was 1986, the peak of the real estate market's boom. Some pundits down in Washington, D.C., decided it was time to rein in a few overzealous developers, who, the pols claimed, were unfairly taking advantage of tax breaks and favorable depreciation schedules. The 1981 tax code was revised, and the Tax Equity and Fiscal Responsibility Act of 1986 (TEFRA) was passed, destroying just about any incentive anyone might have for investing in real estate. And, you may remember, it included a stipulation that the tax laws be applied retroactively. Overnight developers and investors went bust by the thousands. The banks did just as badly.

Here's why. First, TEFRA eviscerated the tax shelters—in place to encourage investment—thereby leaving investors virtually no incentive to put their money into any type of development—including low- and moderate-income housing. Second, the upper-income tax rate was lowered from 51 percent to 32 percent. Investing involves risk. With a 51 percent tax, investors might take a chance on a new housing project. If the project went south, the investor could recapture his losses in the form of a tax break. If an investor is taxed only 32 percent, why bother with the risk?

The most damaging effect of this law was, of course, that it would be applied retroactively. Property values fell so precipitously that developers who had never missed a loan payment were being foreclosed upon because regulators, pointing to the abruptly devalued worth of their mortgaged property, demanded millions more in additional collateral. I couldn't believe that a government would allow deals to be made and then wipe them out. It's one thing to establish a new set of guidelines; it's another thing to say, *Guess what, the rules you were playing by, and basing already done deals on, are dead.* Some people had to pay for tax shelters while, at the same time, paying taxes on the shelters they were buying. Most surprisingly, while I can understand politicians doing the wrong thing, I couldn't believe that the retroactivity provisions would be upheld by the courts, but amazingly, they were. It was a total disaster and incredibly unfair.

People don't seem to understand this (and apparently members of the Supreme Court don't either), but in terms of economics, real estate is the backbone of this country. The industry alone accounts for 20 percent of the gross national product, employs eight million workers, and generates $200 billion in tax revenues. Construction not only creates jobs, it spurs manufacturing. And consider the retail aspect: If people buy houses, they buy carpets, furniture, and so on.

These politicians—many of whom had never functioned in the world of big business, or any business, for that matter—couldn't see past their fingertips. They passed this thing into law without giving one thought to the long-term consequences. Witness the domino effect: By 1993, 62 percent of all airlines had gone bankrupt. Fewer houses were under construction than in 1946. Not since the Great Depression were so few construction workers employed. The Resolution Trust Corporation was forced to sell its property at five cents on the dollar. Real estate values sunk trillions of dollars during this time. Imagine my despair as I watched every single asset I owned—condominiums, hotels, casinos, my airline—hit the skids.

One day, while walking down Fifth Avenue, hand in hand with Marla, I pointed across the street to a man holding a cup and with a Seeing Eye dog. I asked, "Do you know who that is?"

Marla said to me: "Yes, Donald. He's a beggar. Isn't it too bad? He looks so sad!"

I said, "You're right. He's a beggar, but he's worth about $900 million more than me." She looked at me and said, "What do you mean, Donald? How could he possibly be worth $900 million more than you?"

I said, "Let's assume he's worth nothing (only from the standpoint of dollars)—I'm worth minus $900 million."

This was an interesting period of time, because as I told the story I realized in my own mind that what I was saying was true. I also began to realize that I had better get back to work!

My net worth had been in the billions. By the spring of 1990 I was deeply in the red; my empire was hemorrhaging value. When the Supreme Court upheld the retroactivity provisions in 1992, I knew that not only for me, but for my colleagues as well, prospects were

grim. Even for the awesome Olympia & York, headed by the powerful Reichmann family, the future looked bleak.

I remember reading about the trials and tribulations of Paul
Reichmann and his O&Y empire. The company owed a staggering
$20 billion and was in deep, deep trouble. Its investments were shaky,
and getting shakier all the time. It was unthinkable that O&Y could
be going down, but it sure as hell seemed that way by reading the
papers.

Paul Reichmann made a huge error: He let his ego get in the way
of his financial recovery. I remember the day I knew his end would
come. I picked up the paper and read a "death knell" story about
O&Y, and Reichmann was quoted, saying O&Y still had a net worth
of $5 billion. First of all, this probably wasn't true. Second, if you have
$5 billion, why in the world would banks pity you and discount your
debt? Forget it! I guess Paul just couldn't put his ego aside for a second
and tell the banks how much trouble he was really in. It ended up
hurting him badly. The company, as we knew it, was totally wiped
out. And Reichmann was left holding the bag.

I wasn't quite at that point yet. But I was close. The casinos in
Atlantic City weren't throwing off enough cash to service the debt. I
felt trapped. So in March of 1990 I told Wall Street I might miss
Trump Castle's $43 million principal and interest payment. This
announcement reverberated around the world because I had never
missed any payment before. Suddenly bankers—some I'd worked
with for a decade—were doubting my ability to make upcoming payments on my other loans. They were right to be skeptical. I wasn't sure
myself where the money would be coming from. The problems at the
Castle could have triggered a series of defaults, forcing me into personal bankruptcy. And there was no way Donald Trump was going
bankrupt! I would talk about bankruptcy and I would use that possibility as a tool to negotiate, but I'd never do it. That would end the
game.

So I dug in. I waited—waited and watched. I took tremendous punishment as I watched my empire collapsing around me. Finally, it became obvious to me and the rest of America that the economy was crashing for all. When this realization hit me, I decided I'd do everything in my power to suffer the pain as early as possible. Negotiate, I thought, before everyone else starts getting into the game. I now realize that, if I had waited just six months longer to renegotiate terms with the banks, I might have lost everything, because six months later I would have had to stand in line with a whole bunch of other moguls who were trying to do the same thing—work out a deal, get a discount on debt, buy some time. In retrospect, that decision was perhaps the smartest thing I did.

Sure, it crushed my ego, my pride. I hated having to go to the bankers with my hat in my hand. And yes, my lifestyle was a little cramped for a while. I guess all that's important. But getting a deal on the table—without filing for bankruptcy—was the most important thing of all. I decided there was no way I'd make the same mistake Paul Reichmann had made—I wasn't going to let my ego get in the way. I figured I'd sell off a few assets and suffer a small hit to my ego in order to keep my 18,000 employees and kept afloat the thousands of family firms and suppliers that were dependent on the Trump Organization for work. After all, these people would have found it much tougher to recover. I wouldn't have been able to look in the mirror if I'd let them down.

I knew I had to protect myself—by being flexible. I never get attached to one deal or one approach. I keep a lot of balls in the air because most deals fall out no matter how promising they seem at first. This was particularly important now, since after I missed the Castle payment, the bankers involved in my loans would certainly get more involved. I was fortunate enough to work with some tremendously talented people: Ann Lane of Citibank, Joe Manganello of Bankers Trust, and Peter Ryan of Chase Manhattan, to name a few.

They were big-picture types—not middle-management bureaucrats lost in the minutiae. They often shared my vision, and they brought to the table much vision of their own.

I dealt with some real jerks also. One was named Ben Berzin, who worked for Midlantic Bank. He sometimes gave more than you ever thought you could get, and sometimes gave nothing when it wouldn't have mattered to him. He was an amazing phenomenon. I cut a deal with him on a loan in Atlantic City that was secured by a casino property, much of it guaranteed by me. The discount was tremendous. Frankly, I was a little surprised I was able to get so much out of him. During this period Berzin acted normal and seemed very calm.

But after he made the deal, he turned into a monster. For the smallest nothing he would threaten to issue a default notice. Berzin would call up and scream at people at the top of his lungs about nonsense, and yet he gave me tens of millions of dollars in discounts. After I was finished with this jerk, I called him to ask why, with his attitude, he made the deal in the first place, and after having made the deal, why he was so obnoxious? He really had no answer.

I knew—and I think he knew, in the end—that if he'd just sat back with me, as I had originally asked him to do, he would have been paid out in full. Instead, I am proud to say, he lost a lot of money on the transaction.

I recall my first meeting with Berzin; it was very strange. He brought me into his office, and suddenly he started smiling. He showed me a plaque of a golf ball and golf club and happily told me this long story of how he'd foreclosed on the developer of this club. How he'd taken the club away from the guy. I asked him if the developer was hurt, what kind of a guy he was. Berzin didn't know; he didn't care. All he knew was he'd "beat this guy into the ground." I knew immediately what kind of jerk I was dealing with. Had I not made my deal with him at the beginning, he would have been impossible to deal with at the end. He was a huge detriment to the bank.

On my loan alone, I believe he could have gotten the bank tens of millions of dollars more.

Another banker who was incredibly disappointing to me was Patricia Goldstein of Citibank. She's a tough, hard woman with very little social grace. She's not well liked by those who know her, and she's particularly disliked within the real estate industry. Because she has Citibank on her shoulders, she thinks she's hot shit. And believe me, she's not.

I'll never forget the time, during my ongoing struggle, that I got a call from Pat crying hysterically into the phone. She told me that her husband was dying. He was being cared for at a hospital somewhere in the Bronx where, she said, they were treating him horribly. Was there anything I could do, she asked, to help get him into Mary Manning Walsh, a home for the terminally ill run by the Carmelite sisters and the Catholic church? It is also a place that is virtually impossible to get into. I called a good friend, who called the cardinal, who in turn called the bishop of New York, and essentially I worked like hell to get her husband into a place that was harder to get into than the Wharton School of Finance. The next day I received a call from the bishop asking me if Mrs. Goldstein could be at the hospital at six o'clock in the morning for a tour and if the husband could be brought in immediately. Mr. Goldstein was admitted and, for the rest of his life, had nuns hovering over him, praying for him, taking care of him like no one did before.

Not only did Pat Goldstein never even thank me, but as hard as it is to believe, when I dealt with her she was nasty and mean. To top it off, she made a truly stupid deal for Citibank. Had she listened to my advice about the Plaza Hotel, the bank could have made hundreds of millions of dollars more than it ended up making. But she wouldn't listen to anybody. And the fact that I helped her in the most important way meant absolutely nothing to her. She tried to screw me at every corner. As a result, she prevented the bank from being able to take advantage of a great situation.

I will never forget the day I was forced to call the banks to renegotiate my loans. This was something that I never thought could happen to me. It was awfully tough when you had come from the top—and had been there so long. I called a meeting. Most of my major banks were there, and my conference room was packed. I told them, in as nice a way as possible, that I was in deep financial trouble and that, on top of that, I wanted more money, about $65 million. Their jaws fell to the floor. Their eyes glazed over.

After the initial shock had worn off, we began to talk. Some were angry; all were concerned. But this was very early in the process. The reason I wanted the $65 million, I said, was that my business was good, but there was no liquidity in the markets. My projects were great, unlike a Canary Wharf that was sucking O&Y dry. They were well located, with well-built, magnificent buildings. I hadn't incurred cost overruns or the other problems attendant to most properties. What I did have, I explained to the dropped jaws in front of me, were great properties in a terrible market. The asset values had dropped precipitously, but the borrowings had not. In 1989, with approximately the same debt, I had a net worth of almost $2 billion, maybe more. By the end of 1990 I had the same debt levels, but I was in the red. The problem: property values had plummeted so dramatically that many of my projects were worthless. In retrospect, it all seems easy to understand. Nevertheless, at the time, it was one of the toughest meetings I've ever had.

Essentially, I placed a big bet. "Look," I said. "I can tie you guys up for years—in court proceedings, bankruptcy filings, and the other legal maneuvers I'm good at—when forced. But I'm willing to do something else." I told them that if they gave me a $65 million line of credit, used only to keep my valuable assets and good business going, I'd agree to end any thought of legal skirmishes. My side of the deal looked like this: First, the banks would float me $65 million to keep my head above water. Second, no single bank could lay claim against me for five years (until June 30, 1995). Third, all interest and principal on loans would be deferred until that time. It was a win-win situation for all. I was able to buy some time in hopes that the casino or the real estate markets would rebound. And the banks were able to collateralize their unsecured debt and consolidate the rest.

This was the biggest bet of my life, and boy, did it pay off! Had I tried to make this deal six months later, it would have been impossible. The banks were becoming more and more illiquid—there's no way they would have been able to allow any more money to go out. They were as tight as I was then. Timing, once again, was everything.

The short of it is, the banks got smart. In order to save the vast amounts of time and money entailed in what would have been one of the most complicated proceedings ever, the banks more than capitulated—they enthusiastically agreed to my proposal. I kept my business going; I had liquidity. And I never took down more than $45 million of the $65 million credit line. I started paying off one loan after another. I was working like never before.

While I had my miscues with some bankers, I also earned a respect for bankers in general. Some of the people I dealt with were as smart and cunning as you can imagine; they were also good people. Some of them, such as Manganello, Ryan, Ann Lane, Peter Bauman, Tony Terracciano, and Steve Busch, would do well wherever they went. And I really owe them a lot, not only for their wisdom, but for their flexibility and understanding.

It was three o'clock in the morning when Ann Lane of Citibank called me and said, "Donald, sorry to wake you up, but can you get up and immediately come to our war room? We're having trouble with three banks—one in Austria, one in Japan, and one in Singapore. We think you should be here to talk to the presidents of the banks yourself. If we don't get them, the whole deal will collapse because we must get all ninety banks, unanimously." At 3:15 A.M. on a cold, wintry morning with sleet falling from the skies, I got up and walked ten blocks to Citibank—my driver was at his home, and so, I guess, were the rest of New York City's taxicab drivers. I arrived drenched and cold. I turned to Ann and said, "This is a new low point." Anyway, Ann's a star—she's the one who guided Rupert Murdoch through his troubles at Citibank, which launched his tremendous comeback and success. She met me with an army of assistants. We placed the calls, one by one, and I was able to convince the banks to do what was in their best interest and also in mine. I may have been successful, but it certainly wasn't fun.

This was one of the most complicated transactions of the nineties. Ninety banks had billions of dollars in debt. I will always remember the morning of June 30, 1990. I arrived at the law offices of Weil, Gotshal, Manges & Rosen at 8:00 A.M. There greeting me—stacked two feet high and spread across every inch of their largest conference table—were two thousand documents, all of which needed my signature. I started signing. The clock hit 10:00 A.M. Wait, I asked some associate, where is my lawyer? The partner I had dealt with for the past fifteen years was an old friend and a confidant. I couldn't believe he wasn't there at eight—and here it was ten? The clock hit noon. Where is he? I asked again. Another associate told me he was in meetings. It took me two days to sign all those documents, and this guy finally showed up. Fifteen years of deals, fifteen years of business—and he shows up late. He regrets that now! And he has paid a big price with me. Anyway, it was the best deal I ever made.

One thing I learned from all this: Sometimes the best thing you can do is just let things ride, let time go by. There were moments when I felt bored, useless, like my hands were tied. I wanted to do something! But the truth was, a lot of the negotiating that took place didn't really have much to do with me. It more involved huge conference rooms of midlevel bankers quibbling over millions of dollars of secured and unsecured debt. They could certainly do this without me. It was mainly out of my control.

Me with Greg Norman and Nelson Peltz—we had just won Greg's charity tournament.

As a result, I had a lot of time on my hands. That's when I decided I'd take up golf again. It helped me relax and concentrate. It took my mind off my problems; I only thought about putting the ball into the hole. And it certainly beat hanging around the office waiting for my phone to ring. Why sit around the office bugging people on the phone—or having people bug you—when you can get some sun, relax, and take your mind off your problems? The irony of this, of course, is that I made so much damn money playing golf during those months.

I remember one Sunday, in particular, when it looked like things were really coming to an end. One banker truly hated me and was looking to cause lots of trouble. My lawyers that weekend were drawing up nasty papers, and so was his bank. It looked like it was going to be a very, very big fight, which, ultimately, would have been bad for

With Tiger Woods: If this guy keeps it up, he'll be worth more than me.

both of us. I was hitting balls on the range and didn't really feel like going out to play when a friend of mine came over and said, "Would you like to play golf with so-and-so?"

"Wait a minute, Dan," I replied. "Isn't he the head of Bank X?"

The answer was yes. "Does he know that you're asking me to play golf with you guys?" I asked.

"No, he doesn't. But why would there be a problem?"

"Look, if you go back to him and say that it's me and he still wants to play, I would find that very interesting."

My friend told the banker, who looked up, nodded, and said begrudgingly, "Let's play."

The round started off very badly, in that the banker was unable to get his ball airborne. He played two or three holes terribly.

I said to him, "Look, your grip is really bad, and if you could just move your hands over, I think you'd be a much better player." I repositioned his hands and he started hitting the ball better than he had ever hit it before. With just that one minor change, he actually became a good player. He never had a better time and even went to the driving range afterward to practice with his new grip. More important, he thought I was a nice guy, not the vicious, flame-throwing jerk he had envisioned. He couldn't believe it. As we were leaving the course he said to me, "Look, I know we're going to war tomorrow, but maybe we could make a deal." I laid out the terms of a deal that would be fair to all, and he agreed. The next morning his lieutenants, who had until that point been totally vicious, called my people and informed them that a deal had been made and to get the paperwork done. We signed the next day, and hundreds of millions of dollars' worth of problems went away. Just like that. Pfff!

Just for some contrast, I'll divulge this tale: I once saw Jack Nicklaus, and I told him, "You know, Jack, I've actually made much more money playing golf than you have." He didn't really understand what I meant, nor did I explain. But he probably went away thinking I'm a real jerk.

Boxing, like golf, is a microcosm of life in its raw competitiveness, its unpredictability. Boxing, like business, is do or die. One of the greatest boxing matches I've ever seen was between Julio Cesar Chavez and Meldrick Taylor. There's no question about it that pound for pound Chavez was the greatest fighter around. His 82–0 record was proof of that. Julio was a craftsman, a workman. When he got into the ring, he would immediately immobilize his opponent, then destroy him. Meldrick Taylor, on the other hand, had a reputation for being fancy, quick, and beautiful to watch in the ring. During their now legendary fight, Meldrick danced around the ring, getting shots in whenever he could, while Julio, not looking quite so pretty, inflicted tremendous damage. In the twelfth round, realizing how close the match was, Meldrick made a huge mistake. Instead of dancing through the last round and, possibly, through speed and quickness, winning the fight on points, he decided to mix it up with Julio.

Until his fight against Mike Tyson, Evander Holyfield was always thought of as a great light-heavyweight champion; he was never really a heavyweight. Now, after pummeling Tyson, he is considered one of the greatest heavyweight champs ever.

He was one of the greatest champions of all time. Unfortunately, Larry Holmes came after Muhammad Ali, and was forced to box in his shadow.

This is a terrible strategy. When you're doing well, maybe even winning, against somebody who remains unbeaten after ten years, you don't try to knock him out. History had already proven Julio a champion. But in the final round these two great warriors went to the middle of the ring and just started banging. Incredible amounts of pain were being inflicted on Meldrick, and people in the audience were wincing. He started to back up. His legs got weak, and Julio got him against the ropes, continuing to beat him unmercifully. They stopped the fight with only a few seconds left, and Julio won. Meldrick Taylor will never get another chance at Chavez—that fight seemed to end his career as a real boxer—but if he does, there's no way he'll make the same mistake again.

By 1993 I began to feel more like Chavez than like Taylor. My personal debt of $975 million had been reduced to $115 million, and I had two years to finish cleaning it up. There was no way to deny that things were going really great. Piece by piece, deal by deal, a beautiful picture was beginning to emerge. What my people and I had already achieved was astonishing.

I began to prosper a long time before the newspapers and other media acknowledged it. Apart from realizing my modest success, the media was, in fact, gleefully predicting my collapse—at a time when I knew I was coming on strong. This went on for about two years. I call it the period of the unknown. I sold some assets—my yacht, the Trump Shuttle, and a few others—but for the most part, I kept everything I'd had in the first place, and just reduced debt. Thinking back, it's really amazing that today I'm worth much more than I was in the eighties. I have mostly the same assets and many more. The company is far bigger and doing better than it ever did before.

TRUMP COLLECTION/SKYVIEWS

A view of Atlantic City—which does more business than the entire Las Vegas strip.

REBUILDING THE BOARDWALK:

TRUMP'S NEW SKYLINE

WHEN PEOPLE LOOK AT MY SKYSCRAPERS IN NEW YORK, they often ask me why I even bother with Atlantic City. The fact is, the only people who ask this question are those who have never gone to Atlantic City. They've never seen how massive it is, never seen the millions of people who pour in weekly, never seen the kind of action and excitement you can't find anywhere else.

If truth be known, without Atlantic City, it is highly unlikely that Random House would have asked me to write this book, because it was the tremendous cash flows from Atlantic City that allowed me, unlike many other real estate guys, to escape the tough times of the early 1990s.

I remember when one of the greatest real estate men of them all, Larry Fisher, the head of Fisher Brothers in New York, read that the Taj Mahal had cost over $1 billion to build. He couldn't understand it. He's a friend of mine, so he called to ask, "How the hell could a casino cost this much to build?"

Larry hadn't been to Atlantic City and therefore had not seen how the Taj dominates its skyline. I tried to explain what it looked like. He couldn't believe it. He was envisioning a small hotel with a few slot machines and a couple of table games. For that I would have thought a billion dollars in cost would have been nuts, too. When I got off the phone, I knew Larry was still in the dark. "You really have to see it to believe it," I told him.

A couple of months later I got a call from Larry. He was in his helicopter, traveling down to Atlantic City. He yelled over the roar of the propellers: "I'm circling over the Taj Mahal. Now I understand what you're talking about. I finally get why it cost a billion dollars, and I can't believe it didn't cost more. The thing is absolutely amazing."

Atlantic City has always been one of the most underappreciated gaming jurisdictions in the world. More people travel to Atlantic City in a year than to any other destination in the United States. Its twelve casinos do more business than the entire Las Vegas strip, and that includes Caesars Palace, the MGM Grand, the Mirage, Circus Circus, and all of the others. These are two facts nobody seems to understand or even believe—except for the people who go to Atlantic City. And it's only going to get bigger. The smart Wall Street analysts agree with me. Some of the others don't, but let's see who is right in the long run.

My Atlantic City ventures have been well chronicled in my first two books. I'm not going to bore you with details of the complicated and often very tedious meetings that took place in the back rooms of investment-banking houses and law firms. What *is* interesting to note is that I was able to take my great casino empire, which makes me far and away the number-one player in Atlantic City, and bring it through a horrific storm. With the help of Nick Ribis, the president of my casinos, and many others, I was able to survive a terrible time in the financial markets.

We ultimately raised $2 billion in two separate public offerings: $1.4 billion in debt, $600 million in equity. Much of this money was used to repay old debt, bonds, and various other liabilities I had accumulated. In the end, everybody was happy.

My Atlantic City empire is composed of the Trump Taj Mahal, Trump Plaza, and Trump Marina, all of which receive a four-star rating by the *Mobil Travel Guide* and four diamonds by AAA. What amazes people the most is that in a city where there are major players from Las Vegas and the rest of the country, Trump Taj Mahal is the number-one casino and Trump Plaza is number two, a difficult feat. They're near each other and owned by the same company. They compete with each other yet continue to hold the two top spots. The skyline of Atlantic City says TRUMP—just like the skyline of Manhattan says TRUMP.

A lot of characters show up at our casinos. A wealthy Arab, along with a string of beautiful women, once landed in Atlantic City in his brand-new 747. He immediately went to Trump Marina and—for days on end—played simultaneously at two $100 slot machines with a woman on each knee. He gambled millions of dollars over four days. Another guest had a proclivity for cars and, after losing millions of dollars, would often ask for appeasing gifts—Rolls-Royces, Ferraris, you name it. He was always amply rewarded.

Akio Kashiwagi, a Japanese real estate tycoon, was different from both of these men. I had actually met Kashiwagi in Japan at a party I gave for some Japanese friends and investors the night before Mike Tyson's championship fight with Buster Douglas in 1990. When Iron Mike arrived with his entourage, including Don King and his electrified hair, everybody went wild and wanted to have their pictures taken with the champ. I asked Mike if it was all right, and he and I started shooting pictures with some of the guests. As we walked around the room, I spotted Kashiwagi standing in a corner, staring at the wall and talking to no one. I walked over, put my arm around him, and gently shoved Mike into place for the picture. Kashiwagi went completely nuts, screaming, "No picture! No picture!" He put his hands over his face, turned his back on us, and stalked angrily out of the room. Mike and I looked at each other and asked, "What the hell was that?"

Whether it was a coincidence or an act of vengeance I don't know, but the next day Kashiwagi boarded a private plane and flew to Trump Plaza in Atlantic City. Earlier in the year I had had dinner with the late Sir James Goldsmith, the great European tycoon, and he told me about Kashiwagi. Apparently he was one of the biggest and best gamblers in the world—and he bet huge amounts of money. Kashiwagi was a strict rules player, and when he played baccarat he never varied from the odds. In fact, Kashiwagi had recently been down to Sir James's casino in Australia, the Diamond Beach, and had nearly broken the bank when he won $20 million at the baccarat tables. During this period I was beginning to feel the economic pinch and was somewhat reluctant to play a guy who was known to bet $250,000 per hand. *Every* hand. But I couldn't help thinking that it would be pretty spectacular if I won.

When Kashiwagi arrived, my people met him at the airport with a limousine and whisked him directly to Trump Plaza's presidential suite, where he sat for two days without moving. When he finally arrived at the casino on Friday night, thousands of chips in the highest denominations were placed in front of him. The stacks, worth $250,000 each, stood over a foot high. The action started immediately, and from the very first hand, Kashiwagi started beating the hell out of us. Within the first half hour I was down a million dollars, and not long after that I was down $2 million. I thought about my conversation with Sir James. What the hell am I doing? I asked myself. Cash flow is way down, and I'm playing with a guy who could win $40 or $50 million in a matter of days.

Baccarat is a great game for the gambler because the house has very little, if any, advantage. In fact, after all of the perks that the high rollers get, you could say the gambler has an advantage over the house. At that moment I realized for the first time that I had become a gambler, something I never thought I was. In the past when people asked me if I gambled, I always answered, "No, I speculate." Because a certain amount of logic and reasoning always went into my decisions. But this had nothing to do with reasoning or logic: I was merely sitting on the sidelines watching as one of the best gamblers in the world played against me for $250,000 per hand, seventy times an hour.

Atlantic City forbade twenty-four-hour gambling back then, so Kashiwagi was forced to stop playing early Saturday morning. But after that first day, he earned himself the reputation among my people for being a warrior. He sat at the baccarat table for eighteen to twenty hours straight without getting up to eat. He didn't even get up to go to the bathroom. He ate rice—but only if it he could eat and gamble at the same time. Surrounded by a crowd of his employees, mostly accountants and statisticians, he was stone cold. He showed no emotion whatsoever.

I, on the other hand, was down by $4 million, and I was not looking forward to Kashiwagi's return. He arrived at 10:00 A.M. I found myself doing something I'd never done before: I called the pit. I had never once inquired about a specific person.

"How are we doing?" I asked.

As it turned out, we were not doing too well. Throughout the next day Kashiwagi continued to win, until I was down $6 million. I hated myself for allowing this guy to come play. This was not the time for me to lose millions of dollars.

I called the pit again. I was told we were down $7 million. Then $7.5 million. Then $8 million. Then $8.5 million.

I stopped calling for a while. A few hours later, I called and we were only down by $4 million. "Great!" I thought. Then I caught myself. How could I be so happy about losing $4 million?

I barked at the manager in the pit, "How'd that happen?"

"We just got lucky, Mr. Trump," he said.

"Did we have the same dealers?"

"No, sir. We had a group of young women dealing to him this time."

The next day Kashiwagi beat the hell out of me again. We were down $9 million. I asked whether or not the three young women were dealing. The pit boss told me no. "It was another crew, Mr. Trump."

The next time I called things were much better. The three women were dealing. They'd whittled his take down to $3 million. Aha, I began to think, a pattern. And that pattern repeated itself, day after day. Until I told the pit boss, "Look, I want those women dealing to this guy all the time."

He laughed. "Oh, Mr. Trump, it doesn't make any difference. It's just a coincidence."

"I don't give a damn if it's a coincidence or not," I said. "I want those women dealing."

I picked up the phone and called all three of them. I let them know that Donald Trump would appreciate it if they would continue to deal to Kashiwagi for as long as it took. In other words, as long as it took to beat him. The women said they would, but they couldn't start immediately.

The next day the men dealt for the last time, and Kashiwagi cooked me badly. He was up $9.25 million. I called the casino. "Look, this guy is killing me. Times are tough enough. Tell him I'm out at ten million."

The pit boss balked. He told me it wouldn't be right.

"Don't tell me what's right or wrong," I barked. "I'm out at ten million dollars—and if we win ten million—not likely at this point—the game is over. Ten and ten. We're out either way."

When Kashiwagi heard my terms, he looked content. After all, he'd be at $10 million—and I mean *up* $10 million—in a matter of hands.

What happened next is something of a miracle. My crew—Dawn Heath, Danuta (Donna) Gruver, Xuan (Swanny) Trinch, Lynn Bradian, and Mun-ching (Melissa) Wy—dealt. They worked their tails off—and beat the crap out of Kashiwagi.

The word was out. Huge crowds formed around the baccarat table as the game got more and more exciting. Then I saw the press.

I recognized a reporter from *The Wall Street Journal.* I was down $9 million. Shit, I thought. I don't need this kind of press. Not at this time. Not now.

I figured the game wouldn't last much longer. I asked the pit boss how we were doing.

I was astonished by his reply: "We're even, Mr. Trump."

Even? How the hell did we ever get even?

"We had an incredible run of luck. Kashiwagi is beginning to crack. I think we've got him now, Mr. Trump."

Over the next ten hours we kept winning until, unbelievably enough, Kashiwagi was down $10 million. Remembering our deal, I told my people to stop the play. Enough was enough. Kashiwagi was not particularly happy about this, but he agreed. Gamblers are honorable, in their own way—at least about gambling. When a deal is made, they usually abide by it.

Kashiwagi went back to Japan. A few days later an article appeared on the front page of *The Wall Street Journal* about his status as the world's most flamboyant gambler. It detailed his stay at Trump Plaza. It explained every move he made—where he went, his personal habits. The story was a disaster for a man who shunned publicity. I later discovered that Kashiwagi was a reputed crime figure. That must have been why he didn't want to be photographed with Mike Tyson. After the article, dozens of photographers surrounded his $30 million house in the middle of Tokyo.

It was a feeding frenzy. One day he completely lost it. He ran outside to get away from two television cameras peering into his window. He tripped over the curb and broke his ankle. His chauffeur pulled him into his black Mercedes and sped off. Kashiwagi went into hiding and was never seen again until his body was found hacked to pieces by a samurai sword. They never caught the killers.

In April of 1990, shortly after Kashiwagi's visit to Trump Plaza, I opened the Taj Mahal, increasing Atlantic City's gaming capacity by 20 percent. With gaming revenues grinding to a halt, this was the worst possible time to bring a new—and huge (the Taj is spread over seventeen acres)—casino on-line.

Acquiring the Taj wasn't something I had planned. In 1987 I bought $96 million worth of Resorts International class B stock for $80 million. Even though this represented only 12 percent of the company's equity, it gave me 90 percent of the vote. I had intended to buy the rest of the public stock for $22 a share so I could take the company private, but out of nowhere, Merv Griffin came on the scene offering $35 per share—nearly a 60 percent premium over my bid. It turns out that Merv didn't have a clue as to what he was getting into (he described it as an "interesting move"), but it was a suicide mission.

There was no way I wished to top Griffin's bid and I decided to negotiate. Our compromise, which gave me $12 million and the unfinished Taj Mahal, turned out to be one of the best deals I ever made. Merv's acquisition of Resorts International—an old hotel/casino in Atlantic City and a resort in the Bahamas—turned out to be the worst deal he ever made. At the time, I thought his chances of making Resorts successful were about as good as his chances of getting Sharon Stone pregnant.

The funny thing about deals is that you never really know, until some serious time passes, who bested whom. It took most people about two years to realize that I had gotten the best of Merv. But he gave me a clue that he'd been bested: He went all around town bragging about the fact that he'd outfoxed me.

When I was going through hard times, Merv gloated over it, not loudly or obviously, but in a more subtle way: "Isn't it too bad about Donald's troubles?" he'd say with a little smirk to anyone who would listen. Merv is a much different kind of guy than people see: Behind his public persona of a sweet, roly-poly, easygoing person, he is really quite something else.

During the Billy Crystal Friars Club Roast at the New York Hilton, Buddy Hackett told a story that pretty much sums up my relations with Merv. He spun an incredible tale. As he told it, he'd run into Merv on the boardwalk while he was performing in Atlantic City. Buddy asked him, "What kind of a guy is Donald Trump?"

Merv replied, "When Donald was born, he was a Siamese twin with a prick in the middle. In order to separate the twins, a great doctor was brought in. When this famous doctor had completed the operation, he went into the waiting room and announced that both twins had died and only the prick was left." Buddy said he thought he'd use this in his performance.

He did. The audience broke up—dying with laughter. I laughed, too. Except I couldn't help thinking that this was probably the way

Merv really viewed me. I'd beaten him badly in business, but believe me, it could have gone either way. Merv couldn't handle it; he couldn't put it behind him.

His smug mug even showed up in *People* magazine. The spin? How Merv had beaten Donald Trump at "The Art of the Deal." I couldn't believe it. Considering his new company had assumed $600 million in existing debt and incurred another $325 million in order to buy the old Atlantic City and Caribbean casinos, it didn't seem he had all that much to brag about. After all, he spent almost a billion dollars on an asset that was already in deep decline. In fact, in 1989 Resorts' projected debt-service bill was over $133 million. The company's estimated cash flow for the same year was a mere $28 million. Do the math.

Ten months after Merv bought the company, Resorts stopped payments on $925 million in bonds. This led to the inevitable bank-

With Mike Tyson and Merv Griffin.

*He's a legendary performer. Unfortunately, Wayne Newton is not as
great with his finances. I've always been there to take his phone calls,
to give advice, and to do anything I can to help.*

ruptcy. Not long after Merv took Resorts into Chapter 11, he gave up
77.5 percent of his equity to the bondholders. In the last quarter of
1993 Resorts lost $44 million, bringing the year's total losses to over
$100 million.

Merv's response? In March of 1994, Resorts filed for bankruptcy
protection. Again. I called it Chapter 22!

Now Merv and I are friendly again. He wrote me a beautiful letter of recommendation on a man who is now running Trump Marina
and doing a great job, John Belisle. I wish Merv the best.

Kevin Costner, Marla, and me: Kevin is a nice guy who is making his own kind of comeback.

When I inherited the Taj Mahal in 1987, I inherited a host of existing problems. Taking charge of a half-finished building wasn't the least of them. They'd already dumped $553 million into the project, a very poorly designed structure, which, I insisted, had to be reconceived. Because of the huge amounts of money already wasted, it would have been foolish, although preferable, to start from scratch. It became a matter of figuring out what had to be changed and what had to be left alone. When I do a project by myself and I am in total control from square one, I always get my projects done on time and under budget.

But the Taj was a disaster area, and the opening date had to be postponed, which was the initial reason behind our cash-flow problems. When we finally opened the Taj in 1990 the economy was terrible.

At the time there was no significant depth in the management of my casinos. With everything going wrong at once there wasn't any time for us to get our bearings. We didn't have the luxury of sitting back and figuring out what was wrong—or even what was working. I started groping around trying to find the best people, but it takes time to put an effectively functioning management team in place, and we didn't have time.

Knowing I needed somebody in charge, I began hiring sycophants, so-called geniuses from Harvard and Wharton. All these kids had ever done was analyze ISLM curves in business school. They didn't have a clue.

Finally, in January 1991, I installed Nick Ribis as my CEO for casino operations in Atlantic City. Initially I was reluctant to hire him. Nick had been my lawyer and friend since 1979. I didn't want to lose him as my personal *or* professional counsel. On the other hand, Nick had a hell of a lot of experience with gaming in New Jersey—he was one of the first attorneys to specialize in gambling regulatory law when gambling was legalized in Atlantic City, and I knew I could trust him.

Nick strongly believed, as I did, that the key to turning the casinos around was finding the right person for each of the properties. Right off the bat he did a search, and within a matter of months we'd hired three of the best hands-on casino operators in the industry.

With the casinos in good hands for the first time in years, Nick and I could concentrate on our long-term debt. Rather than wait for the ax to fall, we decided to take the casinos through a series of pre-arranged restructurings. Restructuring bonds is a complex transaction because it involves not only the banks but also the bondholders and the Casino Control Commission. There are so many people with separate interests that it's hard to get everybody on the same page. Convincing people that a debt reorganization was a good idea was the easy part. A flat-out bankruptcy would have left us with very little chance for recovery. With a liquidation, the worst possible alternative, value drops dramatically and everybody gets hurt. On the other hand, a restructuring could be designed around the core business, giving all parties the greatest chance for recouping any losses. The real difficulty was getting everybody to agree to the same terms.

The Taj Mahal began operating in the middle of an economic situation so bad that almost as soon as the doors opened the Taj's bonds went down considerably in value—along with virtually every other bond in the country. Carl Icahn, one of the toughest, smartest businessmen in America, became a major buyer by taking advantage of this slide (the bonds were trading at about thirty cents on the dollar). When I needed a vote from the bondholders for approval of the Taj's restructuring, I was informed, much to the dismay of everyone around me—especially the professionals on Wall Street—that Carl's stake in my bonds represented a blocking position. His ownership was so substantial that a negative vote by him would almost certainly blow my ability to make a favorable deal. Carl had broken up many deals over the last few years, and in fact, many of the people he'd hurt in business were his friends. The stories of what he'd done to other companies around that time, especially when he had a blocking position, were well known all over Wall Street. George Gilette of Vail and Ben LeBow of Western Union could both attest to Carl's ruthlessness. But none of this mattered to me. In fact, I felt that Carl's presence as a bondholder might even be a good thing for me. Everybody thought

I was crazy, but I know that no matter how tough somebody is, he or she will always remember support you've given or a favor you might have done in the past.

You see, in 1988 Carl had asked me if I would be the chairman of a dinner being held in his honor by the Starlight Foundation, a fabulous charity for children founded by the actress Emma Samms. I didn't really know Carl at the time, but I agreed to do it. A few months later, as the dinner date approached, I called Carl and explained to him that, while it was an honor to be the chairman of his dinner, I would not be able to attend personally. I was in Europe, and the trip back would be impossible. Carl was not happy about this. He told me that all of his friends and family—most particularly his mother—were counting on seeing me. He was very nice about it, but firm. As chairman, he said, I was morally obligated to attend—and he was right. I really had a dilemma on my hands, because my trip to Europe couldn't be cut short. Finally I said, "Carl, is it really that important to you? Because if it is, I'll definitely be there." So I flew back to the United States right before the dinner, which was a rousing success, and left again for Europe as soon as it was over.

Three years later this man was my largest bondholder, and I was not concerned. When the votes were needed, Carl came through in spades. Not only did he vote in favor of my position, but he also helped persuade others—who were not fans of mine at the time—to do the same. The bonds soared, and the bondholders made a great deal of money—including Carl Icahn, who sold his bonds in 1993 for more than twice what he paid for them.

At the completion of the deal I called Carl and thanked him, not only for his support, but for his help in getting others to go along with the deal. "Boy," he said, "are you lucky you came back from Europe three years ago to be with me at my party." In retrospect, I guess that turned out to be one of my better moves. More important, it shows that even the toughest, most hardened businessmen are capable of gratitude.

Once all of the restructurings at the casinos were complete, my aggregate interest obligations decreased from $233.7 million to $132.9 million. I had three stand-alone operations with a full complement of managers and executives. Everything was operating much more efficiently, and there was always the chance that we could refinance in the future.

Through all of my difficulties, I still had my loyal customers, people who believed in me and those who loved my casinos because they are just plain better than the rest. The numbers may have been down, but there was still substantial cash flow and tremendous business. I love my customers because they love me—in particular, they showed their support during the bad times. People would reach for me as I walked through my casinos; sometimes they'd actually grab me.

One time a sweet little old lady reached out to me and grabbed my hand. "Don't worry, Donald," she said. "We're going to be with you. It doesn't matter what's happening now."

Another time I was walking through the Taj Mahal and a lovely-looking woman handed me a lottery slip. "Mr. Trump, I love you and I love your casinos," she said. "I decided to buy this lottery ticket for you."

I asked her how much it would be worth if I hit. She said that the payoff was up to nearly $20 million. I took the ticket, gave her a little kiss on the cheek, and handed it back to her. I couldn't help grinning. "Darling," I said, "you might as well keep this, because twenty million dollars is just a drop in the bucket compared to what I really owe. The banks would gobble up this twenty million for breakfast. It wouldn't even matter."

After dealing with the banks, I turned my attention to the casinos, which were starting to do their best business ever. The value of my real estate holdings was increasing rapidly, and I was beginning to get the feeling that the tough times were ending. Then came the day when I thought just about everything was fixed. Business was great. So I called the folks at Donaldson, Lufkin & Jenrette, or DLJ, one of the most dynamic investment-banking firms in the country, and said, "Let's go. It's time to go public."

At the height of the market, we hit. I raised over $2 billion. I actually could have raised much more, but I chose not to. In retrospect, I'm glad I didn't. Because while my casinos are individually doing very well—much better even than the day I went public—casino stocks have been hit very hard. Wall Street has been tough on us. I find this

JAMES MCGOON PHOTOGRAPHY (ALL RIGHTS RESERVED)

Surveying the West Side Railroad Yards.

somewhat unfair, being grouped with a lot of companies that are fundamentally different. The only thing we have in common is that we run casinos. My company, Trump Hotels & Casino Resorts, is incredibly liquid, with four magnificent casinos, including one in Buffington Harbor, Indiana, right outside of Chicago.

To a large extent, we've all been the victims of Wall Street. There can be a bit of a herd mentality there. Once one analyst starts dumping on an industry, often the others follow. Right now, as I write this chapter, the casino markets have been lousy. They will come back,

A big day in my comeback. Dick Grasso, the president of the New York Stock Exchange—a great guy—and I watch my new issue, Trump International Hotels and Casinos, trade on boards that first day.

Elton John, a truly talented man with an outrageous fashion sense—especially next to my more conservative attire.

though, and the numbers will speak for themselves. I have tremendous confidence in my public company. Those buildings have not been and will not be duplicated, either in location or form. I have tremendous confidence in the future of Atlantic City and my hotels in particular. Time, I believe, will prove me right.

*40 Wall Street: After it was pointed
out to me, I couldn't resist.*

WALL TO WALL—PLUSH:

HOW I GOT 40 WALL STREET

I'M A LIFELONG NEW YORKER. EVEN THOUGH I GREW UP IN the outer boroughs of Brooklyn and Queens, Manhattan has always been my real home. Since I did my first Manhattan deal at the Commodore Hotel, the Trump name has been synonymous with midtown and the East Side. Despite my penchant for uptown, I have always had a special feeling and desire to control one spectacular property in the downtown financial center on Wall Street.

Forty Wall Street is a special building. I've heard people say that it's been overshadowed by the Woolworth Building. Some say it's dwarfed by the World Trade Center. Reality check: Neither can compare with this magnificent 1.3-million-square-foot landmark. Once I set my sights on it, I knew it would be mine. In 1996 I got it. And at my price: $1 million.

Buildings like 40 Wall Street keep me going. I know I'll never get bored. It's seventy-two stories—including the magnificent tower that scratches the sky. The building has had a long and alluring history as a fabled tower often described in books and magazines. For a short time, 40 Wall, which was built in 1929, was the tallest building in the world, soon eclipsed by the Chrysler Building, which, in turn, would be outdone by the Empire State Building. To this day 40 Wall Street is, outside of the World Trade Center, the tallest building in downtown Manhattan. It is perhaps the most beautiful building in New York, and its green copper spire is in a class by itself.

My relationship with 40 Wall Street began as a young man. The moment I laid eyes on it, I was mesmerized by its beauty and its splendor. But I didn't become serious about the building until the early nineties, and at that time it was struggling.

In the 1960s and 1970s, 40 Wall Street was always a fully occupied building. Sprawling law firms and big banks were its primary tenants. It was a hot property.

In the early 1980s, however, it was bought by Ferdinand Marcos, who, as you probably remember, lost control of the Philippines in a brutal and bloody war. Incidentally, Marcos also bought 730 Fifth Avenue, known as the Crown Building, on Fifty-seventh Street, just across from Trump Tower. (You could never say Ferdinand and Imelda Marcos didn't have good taste in real estate.) Unfortunately, during Marcos's reign over 40 Wall, the building suffered greatly. Frankly, who could blame him? What was he going to focus on, a revolution or his skyscraper?

Dealings at 40 Wall became chaotic. It wasn't that the tenants hated the building. Despite its dilapidated state, they loved the location and the views. The problem was that when it came time to renew or extend their leases, it was virtually impossible—due to lack of management and the nagging legal question as to who, in fact, owned the building. Marcos claimed he owned it. But the people of the Philippines claimed Marcos had bought the building with money stolen from them, and therefore, it was owned by the Philippines.

The whole thing was a mess, and Marcos was out. But where there's turmoil, there's opportunity. So half the real estate groups in New York were going after 40 Wall Street. The market was great in the 1980s; Wall Street was hot. There was a virtual bidding frenzy for the building. Jack Resnick and Son, headed by Burton Resnick and his very talented son Scott, ended up buying the building. The Resnicks are a great real estate family, and they descended on 40 Wall Street.

The problem was that the real estate market was beginning to go south; the price the Resnicks paid for the leasehold interest, which was between $100 and 135 million, was too high, the long-term lease was defective, and Resnick was having problems with Citibank.

Through a long, heated, and laborious period of negotiation, it became clear that Resnick and Citibank were not going to make it, therefore 40 Wall Street would be back on the block. I wanted to make my move, but in the early nineties I was in no financial position to do so. The market was terrible, and I was in the midst of straightening out my own finances. That's when I read in *The New York Times* that a group from Hong Kong, the Kinson Company, was buying 40 Wall Street. The price was substantially lower than what Resnick paid. It wasn't that Resnick overpaid; the world was just a different place. At the time, I knew Kinson had made a great deal and I envied them for being able to acquire this jewel.

Nothing is more exaggerated than that ubiquitous real estate expression: "Location, location, location." I've seen people without talent take the best locations and destroy them, losing loads of money in the process. I've also witnessed professionals taking terrible locations and having nothing but success. Don't get me wrong, a good location is a wonderful thing and certainly very important, but if you don't know what you're doing, location alone will not solve your problems. Unfortunately, the folks from Kinson just didn't have a clue.

After things settled down and their purchase was complete, I called them and said I'd like to meet. I wanted to discuss a possible partnership. They came to my office, full of vim and vigor. They didn't seem to be looking for a partner—they just went on and on about their plans for the building. They told me they wanted to gut the lower section of the building and create a large atrium. "Just like Trump Tower," they said.

"That's a wonderful idea," I replied. "But the building wasn't designed for an atrium. The location isn't appropriate for an atrium, and what would you do with the steel columns that are holding up a seventy-two-story building?"

They suggested moving the columns, no matter what it would cost. They seemed convinced that the building would be beautiful in the end.

Well, to tell you the truth, I almost fell out of my chair.

I asked them how their negotiations were going with the owners of the land, the Hinnebergs, a very wealthy German family led by the formidable and highly respected Walter Hinneberg, Walter junior, and Christian. The Kinson people said that they weren't having much luck with the Hinnebergs. They were, in fact, predicting doom, admitting they'd most likely be unsuccessful with their renegotiation of the lease, as Citibank and Resnick had been before them. Although it had sixty-three years to go, the lease was old, and many of the terms were obsolete, making it very difficult to finance. And through the Marcoses, Resnicks, Citibank, and now the Kinson reign, the Hinneberg family had been unfairly maligned. They had gotten a reputation for being impossible to deal with. I'll get to that in a moment.

As the Kinson group was leaving the room, I wished them well and explained to them that they must be careful. Construction in New York is very tricky and expensive, and the project they were getting ready to undertake, particularly removing the columns and underpinnings of a seventy-two-story tower, would be dangerous, complicated, and very pricey. I felt bad for them. It's not that they were stupid or arrogant, they were simply naïve. No one tries to take on structural renovations without a great deal of diligence or study.

I suggested that the building could be magnificent if left alone but enhanced. Unfortunately, they had their minds set on something much different. When they were gone, I shook my head in amazement.

At the time, it seemed like the end of 40 Wall Street. You can imagine my displeasure—such a great, landmark building, such great possibilities, and these guys who had bought it seemed totally intent on going forward with a plan that would take away the majesty of this landmark building—and spending huge amounts to do so.

A number of years went by and the market was not improving. It was, indeed, getting worse. Despite this slump, I kept hearing word that 40 Wall Street—even in as bad a condition as it was—had many leases ready to be signed. Kinson, as it turned out, was unable to sign them because of its difficulties with the Hinneberg family. It was strange. Apparently the Kinson people had poured vast amounts of money into the building but into things you don't see—air conditioning, mechanical systems, and so on. To me this doesn't make sense.

Kinson was represented in the leasing deals by Peter Friedman of the Friedman Realty Group, a high-quality Manhattan brokerage firm. The two guys on the deal, Jeffrey Lichtenberg and Andy Sachs, who now work at Edward S. Gordon Company, told me that at one point they had thirty-six leases ready to go. The problem was, they explained, the leases were just not being countersigned by the Hinne-bergs. I think the Kinson people had never experienced anything like this. First of all, they weren't real estate guys. They manufacture apparel, primarily sneakers, in Hong Kong. That's no background for dealing with the ins and outs of developing in New York. I knew 40 Wall Street could be a success, but not if the landlord refused to sign leases.

As it turned out, not to my surprise, Kinson got a heavy dose of New York. Contractor bills were far more than they should have been. The architect they'd hired—the excellent firm H.O.K—was having a grand time coming up with new and better designs and billing Kin-son millions of dollars. The money Kinson was pouring into the building—tens of millions of dollars—was escalating out of control. At the time I didn't exactly know what was happening. If I had, I probably would have tried to help them. Later on, when I was speak-ing with some of the contractors on the job, they said, "Donald, we're having a field day with these guys." Everybody was making money except Kinson.

Because of my love for this grand building, I'll never forget the day I was in my office at Trump Tower and I received a phone call from a broker named Peter Ng. He told me that the Kinson group wanted to set up a meeting. I immediately knew it was about 40 Wall Street. I knew I'd get it—it was just a matter of time. And now I was going to get it at my price!

Kinson had spent vast sums of money trying to develop it and, quite frankly, they had gotten nowhere. You can't even imagine it. Just the legal problems with the *existing* tenants would have been enough to scare anyone off. But throw in the tremendous difficulties with contractors and suppliers, and basically, they wanted out, and they wanted out fast.

I was thrilled. I invited Peter and his group up to my office. Remember, this would be our second meeting. The same men who had been so full of enthusiasm just three years before were now beaten and depressed by what they had experienced. New York can do that to you. You've got to be tough. You've got to negotiate tough, and you cannot, at any time, let anyone take advantage of you, the way the people had taken advantage of the Kinson execs. Suddenly, word gets out on the street that you're a pushover—or worse—and whoosh! You're history.

As bad as things got for me—and they got pretty bad—I never let anyone push me around. This saved my ass. I always sent out the message: "Don't lie to me. Don't cheat me. Because I'll find out and I'll find you and it won't be pretty." These poor guys were in over their heads. I greeted them warmly: "Welcome to New York." They were not amused.

At this point the market was still bad. It was early 1995, but as the year progressed, I saw signs that things might soon be great. My company was starting to boom.

I'll tell you what was really strange. The Kinson people asked for silence. They said emphatically that they did not want to go out to the market. They wanted to deal exclusively with me. I didn't understand this. In fact, this had never happened to me before. When a market is rising, I go to as many people as possible to see what kind of price I can get. Kinson had tons of contractor liens on the building. This didn't bother me. This is my world. I knew all of the contractors. Some were killers and some were fair, but in every case, they were friends of mine. I had worked with them hundreds of times.

So the negotiations began, what little negotiating there was. I told Kinson I'd pay them $1 million for this magnificent seventy-two-story, 1.3 million-square-foot building. I agreed to assume and negotiate out their liens. My only caveat: I made the deal subject to my restructuring a new ground lease with the Hinneberg family.

They accepted my terms—without a complaint! I was stunned. They just wanted to go home. They'd lost their shirts—vast sums of money—battling in New York real estate. They'd learned a crucial lesson, one I can thankfully say I learned at my father's knee: New York is a minefield, and if you don't know what you're doing, you will get screwed.

So we signed the agreement. Literally, as they were leaving my office (they weren't yet out the door), I put in a call to Walter Hinneberg. I knew the only reason 40 Wall Street had a bad reputation in the real estate community was that everyone knew the legal terms of the ground lease were choking the building. The good news was that the rent—because the lease was such an old one—was incredibly low. I got Walter on the phone in Germany. Even though we were a six-hour time difference and three thousand miles apart, it was an immediate love fest.

Walter is an immensely proud and successful man who hated seeing the stupidity of what was happening to 40 Wall Street. Over the years, he watched as tenants fled the building. Tenants left only because no one knew who owned it or some naïve developers were looking for a quick fix to finishing the building. On the contrary, people like the Kinson folks would spend tens of millions of dollars trying to develop a dream that would never be. Not because they were stupid, but because they were impractical. They didn't have the instincts, the touch.

As soon as Walter and I spoke, he knew what I had in mind.

We worked out a new and modern lease, extending the term from just sixty-three remaining years to over two hundred years. We stabilized the rent, but the terms in the agreement were modernized: Mortgagees would be able to lend, and tenants would be able to sign up quickly.

The new document was fresh and beautiful. I informed Kinson that we had made our deal with the Hinnebergs, and they were astounded. Now it was their turn to fall off their chairs. They never thought anyone would have been able to woo Mr. Hinneberg. What they didn't understand was that the Hinnebergs and their very able real estate representative, Percy Pyne, had a correct vision for 40 Wall Street—long before anyone else.

During this preclosing period, I began to negotiate with some of the contractors who were taking advantage of the Kinson Group. One of them came to my office to discuss a lien, a few million dollars, I think. I asked him, "How have you done on this building? Have you made any money?"

The answer to this question would normally be, "No, Donald, no, no, no! I'm getting killed." This is the only answer, unless the guys are complete idiots. Not this time. They guy looks me squarely in the eyes and says, "Money, Donald, I've made a fortune on this building. Everybody has." He shrugs. I balk. Don't get me wrong, I appreciated his honesty, but I promptly informed him that I would have to take some of that fortune back. He agreed!

In all cases, I settled the liens for a small fraction of the face amount, and I now had one of the best buildings in New York at practically no cost—even before I closed the deal. On top of that, in just a short three months, it was evident to all that the market would soon be strong again. I closed the deal with Kinson and was now the owner, for at least the next 225 years, of 40 Wall Street.

Kinson had wanted $5 million for 40 Wall, which was cheap—only about $4.00 per square foot for a magnificent building. Ordinarily I might have jumped at the offer, particularly because Kinson and its predecessors had poured millions into the building, all of which I would benefit from. However, I recognized there was an even better deal to be made.

For $5 million Kinson would have delivered the building to me free of liens. My attorneys determined that there were about $4.5 million in liens and trade payables against the building, another example of Kinson's total inability to comprehend the operation of New York real estate. I knew that if I paid Kinson $5 million, it would use most of the money to pay off the liens. I couldn't let that happen when I knew I could do a much better job based upon my twenty years of experience dealing with contractors.

I restructured the purchase price in a manner that might give Kinson more cash but would certainly save me millions of dollars. I agreed to pay Kinson $100,000 at closing, with the possibility of paying up to $650,000 more after closing. Kinson was delighted because it did not have to deal with the contractors or worry that the liens might not be released by the closing date. The closing took place on November 30, 1995. Then I really went to work.

Over the next several months I met with many of the contractors and made them very aware that they were no longer dealing with Kinson but with me. By the time I had finished with the contractors, I had successfully reduced the millions of dollars in outstanding liens. My discussions with the contractors turned out even better than expected, as many of them agreed to accept long-term payouts of their substantially reduced claims. All of the contractors agreed to release their liens on the building at the time we agreed to settle the claims, rather than when they were paid in full or got more work. Within a few months of my acquisition of the building, it was virtually lien-free for the first time in many, many years.

As it turned out, following the closing, I was surprised to learn that Kinson failed to disclose to me other claims against the building. Consequently, I elected to satisfy some of those claims from the post-closing amounts Kinson was originally entitled to.

At the end of the day my purchase price for the building was less than $1 million. That in and of itself was an incredible basis upon which to begin my redevelopment of the building. However, as a result of Kinson's intense desire to wash its hands of 40 Wall Street and return to China, I was able to successfully negotiate for peripheral benefits, which eventually resulted in my receiving monies beyond my wildest expectations. For example, at closing Kinson assigned to me certain pending insurance claims for property damage to the building, which it had little confidence in recovering from its insurers. Following the closing, I settled those insurance claims for $400,000. Kinson also assigned to me its rights to pending tax-reduction proceedings involving the years it owned the building. In view of the precipitous decline of the real estate market and the commensurate decline in the value of 40 Wall Street during that period, I have been advised by my certiorari counsel that I may be entitled to a real estate tax refund of as much as $10 million, based upon the assignment of such rights by Kinson to me.

Similarly, as a result of Kinson's unwillingness to remain in this country long enough to pursue claims against tenants for rent arrears, Kinson agreed to assign those arrears to me. Not long after the closing I settled several of those claims for in excess of $350,000. And, most important, I expect to make approximately $20 million per year from the rentals. Not bad for a building that cost me less than $1 million.

So, in 1996 I bought 40 Wall Street, the second-tallest building in downtown Manhattan, for just short of $1 million. After $35 million in renovations, a near-bankrupt building is leasing for as much as $33 per foot, the top of the downtown Manhattan market.

At almost precisely the moment I began my reign at 40 Wall Street, the market began to improve. It was amazing what was going on. A new tax-incentive plan, for both residential and commercial construction in downtown Manhattan, was formulated by Governor George Pataki and Mayor Rudolph Giuliani. It gave huge incentives to investors, taking old office buildings off the market and converting them to residential use. It also gave wonderful incentives to commercial tenants locating or relocating in the downtown area. It was one of the best and smartest tax-incentive programs I have ever witnessed.

The results were immediate. Billy Rudin, of the Rudin real estate family, deserves much of the credit for getting this plan implemented. He had a vision for downtown Manhattan and just wouldn't stop until he made it happen. Every property owner, and indeed the city of New

The Empire State Building. (I own this one too.)

York, owes him a huge amount of gratitude. Billy worked tirelessly to convince the city and state that downtown Manhattan should be given real estate tax incentives for those owners and/or developers who were able to convert old and obsolete office buildings into residential apartments. Not only did this tax incentive take many "dead" buildings off the market at a time when office space was in a terrible state, but it created a frenzy of development and ultimately will make downtown Manhattan very similar in nature to midtown—that is, a twenty-four-hour community where you can live, work, dine, and shop without ever having to leave the area. Billy Rudin; Mayor Giuliani; Fran Reiter, the mayor's talented deputy mayor; Governor Pataki; Sheldon Silver, the assembly speaker; Joe Bruno, the senate majority leader; Charlie Gargano, head of the Urban Development Commission; Joe Rose, the chairman of the City Planning Commission; Carl Weisbrod; Jennifer Rabb; and others deserve a great deal of credit for creating this miracle taking shape before our very eyes. Over the years I have witnessed many tax abatements and tax incentives, some good and some bad, but never have I seen one so beautifully applied and that works so well.

Buildings were taken off the market one by one, as fast as you could count, and the competition for space began to increase geometrically. I had a decision to make. Forty Wall Street was a great building. It offered lots of options. Should I change the use from commercial to residential? I decided to go counter to the trend, as I often do. Almost everybody was taking the older buildings and converting them to residential, but I felt that because 40 Wall Street was so good and so well located, right across the street from the New York Stock Exchange, I would make it the best office building in downtown Manhattan.

My reasons for doing so were twofold. First, I really felt that with the huge incentives given to residential construction, 40 Wall Street would be left virtually by itself, as an office building of the highest quality, for commercial tenants looking for space. Second, it was much less expensive to transform an existing office building—a once high-quality office building—into a new high-quality office building than it was to convert an office building into apartments.

The conversion to office space was going to cost me approximately $60 per square foot. The conversion to apartments would have cost more than twice that amount. Also, in converting to apartments, vast amounts of space (40 Wall Street has huge floors) would have been lost, since an apartment house needs a much smaller "footprint." While 40 Wall Street has approximately 1.3 million feet as an office building, it would have had about 750,000 feet as an apartment building.

Throngs of people fought me on this decision—but not the people in my office. My right-hand man on the project was Abe Wallach, my top real estate guy, who was adamant in his desire to keep 40 Wall an office building. Abe was hugely instrumental in helping me get this deal done in the first place. He's a smart guy and a class act. I feel lucky to have him. My other proponent in this decision was George Ross, one of the most brilliant lawyers in New York. He reminded me that the building had the most outstanding views in the city and was ideal for high-class operations willing to pay big dollars for unique space. George has been crucial in helping to make 40 Wall the huge success that it is.

Perhaps the most pleasurable aspect of 40 Wall Street has happened since its purchase. I decided to call the building the Trump Building at 40 Wall Street, with magnificent bronze lettering atop a new granite façade staring right at the face of Wall Street and directly into the New York Stock Exchange. The lobby has turned out to be a 10—one of my best construction jobs ever.

All other systems in the building not done by either Resnick, Kinson, or Marcos were completed by me. But the money spent by others was so enormous that, other than the cosmetics, there wasn't much left for me to spend. I decided to gut the entire building from top to bottom. Now, when tenants look at the floors, they see vast open spaces, with unparalleled views. The space is renting quickly.

Go down to Wall Street today, and you'll find a crane on every corner. It's beautiful. I hope that everyone who reads this book will be able to visit this majestic area—I believe it to be one of the most romantic settings in New York—and look at the transformation of what was once a proud and great building into an even prouder and greater one. I've had a lot of fun doing it. And the economics added immensely to my enjoyment.

Mar-a-Lago in all of its splendor.

MAR-A-LAGO:

FROM VISION TO VICTORY

MY LOVE AFFAIR WITH MAR-A-LAGO BEGAN IN 1985. I WAS
vacationing in Palm Beach, Florida, and I actually began to like it
down there. During a drive to a dinner party, I asked the chauffeur
what was for sale in town that was really good. He looked at me and
without even a thought said, "Well, the best thing by far is Mar-a-
Lago, but I guess you wouldn't be talking about that."

I asked him what Mar-a-Lago was, and he told me about the great estate and its history. Rather than going directly to the party, I told him, "Drive me over there." Staring at it from South Ocean Boulevard, I realized that it was not only magnificent, but it looked like a project that could be fun. The following day I contacted the various representatives of the foundation that owned the estate and was given a tour. I immediately knew it had to be mine. The walls, the ceilings, the space itself were greater than anything I had ever seen. The house had a grandeur I didn't know existed—certainly not in the real world.

Its 128 rooms, each more beautiful than the one before, sit on the most important twenty acres of land in Palm Beach, the wealthiest community in the United States. Mar-a-Lago fronts on both the ocean and the lake, as the Intracoastal Waterway is referred to. With close to 110,000 square feet of space, Mar-a-Lago is by far the largest house in Palm Beach, even with new 50,000-footers springing up all the time. More detailed and refined than San Simeon, better located than the grand mansions of Newport, Mar-a-Lago has been unrivaled in its beauty and prestige virtually from the time that it was built. My battle for Mar-a-Lago was brutal and endless, a study in determination and patience. At times the odds seemed almost unbeatable, but I hung in, never thinking about giving up. I knew I was fighting for a unique treasure, one with enormous potential and very much worth saving.

On first sight, Mar-a-Lago was like an old, beat-up, overgrown Rembrandt waiting to be restored. I came across the wreckage—a fairy-tale castle built by a kindred spirit, the enigmatic and incredibly savvy Marjorie Merriweather Post. Her haunting past echoed through the halls of the palatial estate—in its sense of the theatrical and the invaluable input of Wall Street wizard E. F. Hutton, her husband.

From 1922 to 1927, the cereal heiress fussed over every detail of the property located between "sea and lake." Three boatloads of Dorian stone were shipped over from Genoa, Italy; more than 36,000

© 1996 ART SEITZ

The view of Mar-a-Lago from above is spectacular. I am amazed at how quickly the hectic pace of New York City can be replaced by this calming vision.

original Spanish tiles were laid (including the infamous "Plus Ultra" panels, which scholars trace to the 1400s—quite a coup). There are more antique Hispano-Moresque tiles in Mar-a-Lago than in any other building in the world except the Alcazar in Spain. It was from Mar-a-Lago that Post ruled Palm Beach society.

It never occurred to me that I'd be in the business of preserving a great historic monument—until I toured the mansion in 1985. I was spellbound by its opulence and detail. I heard the Post Foundation had put it up for sale. I took it upon myself to save it. And I did— despite the odds.

The whole thing started as a lark. Then it became a distraction: It gave me something to do other than play golf on my vacations in Palm Beach. My strategy? I put in a succession of offers; since there were so few legitimate ones floating around, I felt it was the right time to go low. I got it. Some say I got lucky, and others say I just know how to make good deals. I paid the Post Foundation $8 million for the house and grounds, including $3 million for all of the original furnishings—including the china, the crystal, and the goldware. It's hard to believe, but in 1985 that was a record-setting price, yet everyone was shocked because it seemed so low for Mar-a-Lago.

On the Post Foundation sat various members of Marjorie Merriweather Post's family, among them Dina Merrill, Mrs. Post's arrogant and aloof daughter, who was born with her mother's beauty but not her brains. During my fight to save Mar-a-Lago, Merrill would constantly criticize me and say things behind my back, all of which would get back to me. She should have been the one to save Mar-a-Lago. Mommy had given her the money, and it would have been an easy and popular thing to have done. Instead she lives in a terribly furnished Palm Beach condominium, thinking about her failed acting career and how she can make me look as "nouveau" as possible. Other members of her family, however, have stepped up to the plate. Marjorie Post Dye, the granddaughter of Marjorie Merriweather Post, has been a great champion of what I've done at Mar-a-Lago. Marjorie was also a great beauty, a championship swimmer, and from what I've been told, one of Marjorie Merriweather Post's favorite grandchildren. She has spunk and substance. I'll never forget the day I received this letter from her:

Dear Donald,

I have just revisited Mar-a-Lago and I was blown away with the restorative and imaginative quality of what you have undertaken. Of all the Post Family, I love and feel that I am the most intimately identified with this estate. Deenie, priority wise, is more a "Sea Cloud" person. I took my first steps as a baby at Mar-a-Lago almost seventy years ago. I have returned to visit every year thereafter and then I resided permanently in the early seventies to manage the household and staff for my ailing grandmother. My grandmother's fate appeared certain, the future of Mar-a-Lago became, for me, a stressful and unsettling question. Little did I suspect that there was a big, blue-eyed, guardian angel hovering in a holding pattern just waiting to land and take charge. You have saved Mar-a-Lago, and now, as a club it will become alive again and her space has not been compromised by subdivision.

In my heart I feel that you have had the integrity and the class to retain the elegance and style of Mar-a-Lago and so now it is a new and exciting chapter for me as well. Mar-a-Lago could be the "mother" of all clubs. The conversion and updating have shown considerable taste. I was impressed with the ironworks extending up the short second story balcony wall and the additional lighting and fixtures in the patio. It almost looks as if they could have been made by the artisans employed by Mar-a-Lago in the old days. Even the white paint has had a reviving effect as it brightens the interiors. The colorful flowers, the manicured lawns and landscaping, all serve as a magnificent frame for the masterpiece of Mar-a-Lago.

In style, flair and ambiance you are a modern extension of my grandmother's spirit. She told me many times, "Marwee, you are the breath of spring in my life." Now, Donald, Mar-a-Lago can say that to you too.

I am so looking forward to visiting the club upon completion.

With love and many thanks for your hospitality,

Marjorie Post Dye
First Grandchild and Namesake of
Marjorie Merriweather Post

I've never seen anything like the contents of Mar-a-Lago. The furniture and fixtures were, in many cases, absolutely superb. Much of it was retained in my restoration, but the things I didn't like or that were not of the same quality as the rest I sold at auction. Perhaps the worst room was the Tower Suite. It was designed by Dina Merrill in an Art Deco—if you can believe it—motif. The strong Art Deco feeling didn't go with the Spanish-style house, but the furniture, in actuality, was very expensive and had great resale value. At first I didn't know this, then my brother-in-law, Jim Grau, noticed a large Dumpster in back of the house filling up with furniture. "Donald," he said, "you can sell this furniture. You shouldn't throw it away. It has great value. It was designed by Simon Price." He turned out to be right, and we sold it and other furniture for hundreds of thousands of dollars at a Christie's auction. In later years more furniture was sold to make way for the great spa that was being built and the magnificent suites being made out of the so-called servants' quarters. Great collector's pieces have been added to what Mrs. Post already had, and the interiors now are far more beautiful than they were even in Post's heyday.

My first thought on Mar-a-Lago was that it would make an incredible private club. While that may have been my initial thought, and it would have been something great to do, mine is also a world of reality, and I knew that the zoning and local ordinances would never allow such a use. Mar-a-Lago, as impractical as it may have seemed, had to remain a house, or the far worse fate of the wrecker's ball would come to pass; the acreage would be subdivided into large-scale mansion lots. This seems to have been the direction in which many potential acquirers were going. I felt I couldn't let this happen. Mar-a-Lago was too great to allow anything to happen to it that would impact the great beauty that architect Joseph Urban and sculptor Franz Barwick had created.

There's one thing I do that drives my execs nuts: I buy buildings before I know what I'm going to do with them. It's my instinct, my sense that I know it's going to work out. When I bought Mar-a-Lago, I had no concrete plans for its future, but my financial situation in the early nineties put its potential value into sharper perspective. One thing that's become clear to me in the past few years is that you've got to be flexible and open-minded about your assets. That's part of what having vision is all about—finding creative ways to make the best of both good and bad situations.

The neglect that the house and grounds had suffered during the years following Mrs. Post's death had taken its toll. The tennis court was in ruins; the estate was in disrepair. As a matter of fact, the property was known around town as the White Elephant—spectacular, opulent, but impossible to maintain or manage. I knew I had a lot of work to do, but I wanted it. However, unlike other great houses that were sold to military academies and sanitation departments and uses that totally destroyed them inside and out, Mar-a-Lago was virtually sealed and maintained under the loving care of Jim Griffin, whose father had managed the grounds before him, so the deterioration of the estate was not devastating.

I knew immediately it could be brought back to life. Fortunately, the United States government, which had been given Mar-a-Lago as a bequest from Marjorie Merriweather Post to use as the Southern White House, rarely got to use it. Richard Nixon loved the concept of Mar-a-Lago as a place to entertain. He stated to someone during a visit there that he had never seen anything so beautiful. But he had problems to attend to: Watergate. The last thing he had time for was journeying down to Mar-a-Lago to enjoy the sun and fun of Palm Beach. Jimmy Carter, a different kind of guy, thought that Mar-a-Lago was too expensive for the taxpayers and gave it back to the Post Foundation. That's when I stepped in.

I was living happily at Mar-a-Lago with Ivana and the kids. But in actuality, as a house it was far too big. I didn't realize this until later, when I began developing various sections of the house for a club, such as a spa, tennis courts, a card room, et cetera. For many years there were parts of the house I'd never even seen—for example, the bomb shelters. In general, large sections of the house remained vacant and unappreciated. It was only in 1990, at the beginning of my financial crisis, that I thought something would have to be done. The banks liked me, and they knew the "depression" was not my fault, but when you owe billions of dollars, and then you journey down to Mar-a-Lago on your 727 for weekends, it irks them.

I remember sitting in a room full of bankers and trying to work out a very complex situation. In this case, the bankers were friends of mine and were very good people. But I jokingly and stupidly said, "Gee, folks, it's Friday. I think I'll go down to Mar-a-Lago for the weekend."

Sometimes jokes don't go over very well, and this was one of those times. I could see the anger in their eyes as they struggled with my situation. I felt I had to do something, and I had to do it fast. So I said to them, quickly, "Fellows, I'm going to subdivide the seventeen acres of Mar-a-Lago rather than sell the house."

Then I explained: "The house has very little value because it's so big. I'm going to subdivide, save the main house, and build mansions on the grounds. I'll call the project the Mansions at Mar-a-Lago. I'll turn it into a moneymaker."

I had immediately recovered from my faux pas. I made a great situation out of a potentially hazardous one. I tried to never offend my bankers. This time it worked. They were extremely happy to hear this plan because it showed that I was thinking and working. Given that I owed billions of dollars, breaking Mar-a-Lago into a number of housing lots certainly didn't matter much, but it was the thought that counted. I wasn't taking advantage of them.

So I actually did go down with a much different plan in mind: subdividing Mar-a-Lago. I won't soon forget my first meeting with Palm Beach officialdom. Bob Moore, the town building inspector, and Skip Randolph, the attorney for the town, are good and talented men who work very hard to keep the town in sync. I felt that I was entitled to have fourteen lots and that I should have no problem getting them. Both Randolph and Moore suggested a much different scenario: They told me to ask for eight lots, and if I asked for eight, the zoning would go through quickly. This immediately went against

my instincts, against all my hard-learned principles of zoning—
always ask for more than you really want. Even the politicians want
this so that when they cut you back, everyone is happy.

I said to them, if I ask for eight lots, you will cut me later in the
process. They told me no, no, no, eight lots were already approved for
another person who had tried to buy the house but was unable to
raise the money. Can you believe it? Someone else got eight lots on
just a contract, and I went through years of legal skirmishes with the
town of Palm Beach.

Much against my better judgment, my attorney went in, asked for
eight lots, and, after a series of meetings, was told we could get four
or five at most. I knew it. At least I felt good that I had predicted this
would happen! Of course, the town rejected my proposal, even
though it should have been a routine approval. Case in point: Take
adversity and make it an asset. Remember, I stated that Mar-a-Lago
should have always been a club, but never in a million years did I
think it possible to get the property rezoned as a club. A club would
have been the maximum use for the property, and I knew it. Now was
my chance!

First, they'd taken my constitutional right away by not allowing
me to subdivide the land. Why, I thought, would I have to assume
such a burden for the benefit of the town of Palm Beach? It was unfair
and everyone knew it. I was entitled by law to fourteen subdivision
lots. I believe that Bob Moore and Skip Randolph were very embarrassed. Ironically, I think the town council sensed it was making the
wrong move by fighting me so hard. I couldn't have been more helpful. I gave them whatever information they needed. I changed my
plans. It got ridiculous. A number of council members practically
apologized for the rejection, knowing, as they must have, that I was
going to take them to court. I met with the council shortly after their
final vote. Despite the fact that they'd turned me down, it was clear
that they wanted to work things out.

But it was too late for compromises. My team and I reviewed each step we had taken over the past year and a half just to be sure we had complied with every request that had been made of us. Likewise, we examined the actions of the town council and the Landmarks Preservation Commission, and we found plenty of reasons for suing Palm Beach. We filed a $100 million lawsuit on the grounds that my civil rights had been denied. But there was nothing they could do. The town reacted with great anger, and one of the council members stated that if I did not withdraw my lawsuit, they would not negotiate. I told her that I was sorry but it was too late, that there was nothing I could do about it.

At first there was no movement in either direction, but ultimately, the town became concerned. The judge handling the case was not extremely supportive of the town's position. And he was making that quite clear. I would go around asking the council members whether or not Palm Beach would be forced to file for bankruptcy protection if I won the judgment. This did not endear me to them, but it certainly made a point.

During the course of the litigation, while I was doing very well, a member of the town council approached me and said that they would give me the eight subdivision lots. I told them I wasn't interested. I wanted a private club. They came back to me and said that they would give me the fourteen lots, the maximum allowed under the law. I told them I wasn't interested. I reiterated: I wanted a private club. Ultimately, with the help of a new and very talented lawyer, Paul Rampell, and the guidance of two enlightened town-council members, Hermine Weiner and the late M. William Weinberg, the town council of Palm Beach approved Mar-a-Lago for use as a private club. They fought me every inch of the way. But right won out.

One of the principal reasons that I had such strong support from the people within Palm Beach was that, unlike the other clubs in town, Mar-a-Lago would be open to all races, colors, and creeds. Paul Ram-

THE EDITORIAL PAGE

THE TOWN RESTRICTION AGAINST PHOTOGRAPHY AT THE MAR-A-LAGO CLUB IS UNCONSTITUTIONAL AND INFRINGES ON MY RIGHT TO FREE SELF-PROMOTION.

PALM BEACH'S NEWEST CONSTITUTIONAL SCHOLAR

Copyright © 1995 by David Willson. Reprinted courtesy of David Willson.

THIS JUST IN. THE ENTIRE GOVERNMENT OF THE TOWN OF PALM BEACH HAS CLOSED DOWN DUE TO CONFLICTS OF INTEREST WITH DONALD TRUMP.

Copyright © 1996 by David Willson. Reprinted courtesy of David Willson.

pell really pushed this point. The Bath and Tennis Club and the Everglades Club had no Jewish or black members.

Mar-a-Lago would be open to all, and this appealed to a large group of supporters. It also sparked a tremendous fight by those who wanted to preserve the existing system, a system that, in this day and age, seems archaic.

I always knew that the hardest part of making Mar-a-Lago successful as a private club would be getting the approvals. Being admitted to the Wharton School of Finance or Harvard Business School is, in my opinion, far more difficult than staying there. This was the case with Mar-a-Lago. From the moment it was announced that I had won my approvals, people came flocking to the door, wanting to join. I began selling memberships at $25,000 a piece, then $50,000, and now at $75,000. The membership ranks filled up so quickly that even I was astonished. The fight with the Palm Beach Town Council goes on, and I feel strongly that this is because of the discriminatory ways that are prevalent within Palm Beach, but it's now only small battles. The war was won when they gave me my approvals for this great private club.

This interesting anecdote displays a touch of that Palm Beach hypocrisy. During my fight for the private-club approvals, I met with two of the town fathers, whose names I certainly will not reveal. We gathered one afternoon—the two town fathers and their wives. Apparently their wives were traveling to New York together later that afternoon. We discussed the merits of the club, and then I invited them to a party at Mar-a-Lago that night. I told them that there would be close to a thousand people present, among them, I joked, the most beautiful women in the world. They looked at their wives sheepishly, and then they looked at me in horror.

"Oh, no," they each said separately. "We couldn't go to that. We wouldn't even think of going to such a party."

I thought that would be the last I heard of them. But no sooner had I arrived at Mar-a-Lago—a mere ten minutes later—than the two gents were on the phone telling me that their wives had left for New York and that they would love to come to the party.

"Are the girls really going to be that beautiful?" they asked.

Mar-a-Lago has fabulous entertainment. During the past two seasons I've had Celine Dion, Jackie Mason, Julio Iglesias, Diana Ross, the Beach Boys, Tony Bennett, and many others. I offer the best performers in Florida. In fact, a person who is involved with the Kravis Center said to me once, "Hey, Donald, how do you get these great entertainers? It's unbelievable!" The fact is, they come because I ask

The great performer Tony Bennett and me. He's showing off his second great talent—painting!

TRUMP COLLECTION/DAVIDOFF STUDIOS

TRUMP COLLECTION/DAVIDOFF STUDIOS

Celine Dion onstage at Mar-a-Lago. Her great voice added to the atmosphere as I watched her charm the audience with her beauty and grace.

them to come. I have built up friendships with them over the years. I'll say, "Hey, Tony, do me a favor—play Mar-a-Lago next month." And you know what? We're old friends. He'll just say yes, and he'll do it.

One of my most interesting Mar-a-Lago experiences involved the turmoil over Michael Jackson and Lisa Marie Presley. Michael was a friend of mine and a very good guy—but very different. It began in New York, when I got a call from him one day, saying he would be coming to the city and would like to get together. He often called to say hello when he came to New York. This time I invited him out to

Le Cirque, one of the great restaurants of New York, headed by a master, Siro Maccioni. He was very nervous about going to a restaurant; in fact, he said, he hadn't been to a restaurant in years. I found this hard to believe, but after we arrived, I could see that it was true.

This was in the early nineties, at the height of the Michael Jackson madness, and I don't believe I've ever seen a star as hot as Michael was at that time. When Michael, Marla, and I walked into Le Cirque, some of the biggest people in the universe were seated having dinner. These are people who have seen it all. They are rich, they are spoiled, and they are snooty. I will never forget as Michael sat down in his red

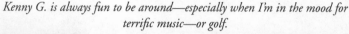

Kenny G. is always fun to be around—especially when I'm in the mood for terrific music—or golf.

Diana Ross—she really wowed the Palm Beach crowd.

military outfit with a large black hat and picked up the menu. It was as if he had never seen a menu before, and we carefully went over each item. But what was most amazing were the looks on the distinguished faces in the room as they came over to our table practically begging for an autograph. These are people who had probably never asked for anyone's autograph before, and I can guarantee you, it was not easy for them to do. They would always start by saying, I have a son who is a big fan of yours, Mr. Jackson. Could you give him an autograph? But I believe it was for them, not their sons. One woman, one of the most socially prominent in New York, known for her attitude, approached our table trying to look cool, then slightly tripped. She grabbed the table for support and asked in the same breath, "Mr. Jackson, can I have your autograph?" It was amazing to see this woman, whom I have known for years, so flustered and nervous.

Somehow, Michael feels comfortable with me. I asked him how he was doing, and we started talking about his life, including his sex life. I was somewhat surprised when Michael told me he had a new girlfriend. I congratulated him and asked, Who is it? He was very shy and looked down into his napkin, then put the napkin over his face and said, "Trump, Trump, I don't want to talk about it, I'm so embarrassed."

I chided him. "Come on, Michael," I said, "tell me who your new girlfriend is." When he finally looked up, he said that it was a girl named Lisa Marie. That was the end of the conversation, and we went on to another topic.

A couple of weeks later, I got a call from Michael asking if he could go down to Mar-a-Lago with me. I said absolutely, and we flew down in my plane together. Michael had a small group of people with him. We did a lot of talking. On the flight down, he asked if it would be possible for his girlfriend to come over and say hello and even stay at Mar-a-Lago with him. I said absolutely, I looked forward to meeting her. I asked if it was the same girl, Lisa Marie. He said yes, it was, and she would be arriving sometime around eight o'clock, about an hour after we got to the house.

When the doorbell rang, the butler answered, and a beautiful girl walked through the door. I don't believe people realize how pretty Lisa Marie Presley's face really is. She's got the best of Elvis and Priscilla, and I don't think she has ever been recognized for her incredible glow. In any event, Michael came running down to the living room, greeted her with a hug, and then took her off to look at the ocean. When they came back, holding hands and hugging, they seemed very much in love. I'm not saying that I was surprised at this, but there was no doubt in my mind that they definitely had something going.

During the weekend we saw very little of Michael and Lisa Marie, since they stayed up in the tower. Then they made the mistake, on a Saturday afternoon, of trying to sneak out of Mar-a-Lago and go shopping, in disguise, on Worth Avenue. Well, the paparazzi found out, and all hell broke loose. They were driven in a limousine back to Mar-a-Lago with the paparazzi in pursuit. The rest of the weekend was absolutely wild. Hundreds of cameras surrounded Mar-a-Lago as Michael Jackson and Lisa Marie Presley were stationed in their love-nest tower rising high above the house. The press didn't bother them, or me either, but it was quite a frenzy.

I had other guests at Mar-a-Lago, one of them the brilliant New Jersey businessman Arthur Goldberg. He took a company named Bally, which was in tremendous trouble—by any other account should have been bankrupt and defunct—and through sheer talent, energy, and force built it into a great company in a short time, and sold it to Hilton Hotels for $3 billion. Arthur made over $100 million on the transaction, and I often cite him as one of the few examples I have seen of a top executive truly deserving what he gets. He did an absolutely incredible job. He is now the president of Hilton's gaming division and is working closely with Barron Hilton and Steve Bollenbach.

Performer-extraordinaire Michael Jackson with my two kids Ivanka and Eric in the Great Hall.

In any event, Arthur and I were having a meeting in one of the rooms at Mar-a-Lago when there was a knock on the door. Arthur didn't know Michael Jackson was staying at the house, but he was aware that there was a great commotion and he was curious as to why there were so many people outside taking pictures. Arthur got up to answer the door. This particular room at Mar-a-Lago, the Dutch Room, is done in very dark woods and is lit very dimly, in keeping with the look. Arthur swung open the door, and there was Michael Jackson. Arthur couldn't believe it. "Look, look, it's Michael Jackson," he said to me. Michael, on the other hand, saw somebody he wasn't familiar with, put his hand over his face, and ran down the hallway. That was the last we saw of Michael that weekend. He went back up to the tower to be with Lisa Marie.

People often ask me whether or not the relationship was a sham, and I give them an emphatic no. I was there, and the magic of Mar-a-Lago brought it out, because after they left, it didn't work so well. I can tell you, for at least a period of time, these two folks were really getting it on.

I think Mar-a-Lago will transcend me. And I like it much better now than I did as a private house. Then I was bored. As I said before, vacationing does that to me. Now, on the weekends, I'm not just screwing around playing golf. I'm creating a masterpiece, something people can really enjoy for years to come.

Trump International Hotel and Tower.

TRUMP INTERNATIONAL:
FOUR-STAR LIVING

I OWE JACK WELCH, DALE FREY, AND JOHN MYERS OF GE a great deal. Jack Welch is the brilliant and legendary chairman of GE who, some twenty years ago, steered GE on a path that made it just about the biggest and strongest company in the world. In my book, and in the books of many others, Jack Welch goes down as one of the greatest business executives of the last century. Dale Frey was the head of the $56 billion GE pension fund, GE Investments. Dale is a rough-and-tumble guy with incredible instincts who just always seems to get it right. John Myers was Dale's assistant at the time and, rightfully, replaced Dale as the head of GE Investments after Dale retired in January of 1997.

These three men together did something that very few executives, especially executives of such a huge institutional company, would have done. They chose me to develop one of the most important parcels of real estate in New York, a parcel owned by GE and located at an address I would rename One Central Park West. It would became known as Trump International Hotel and Tower.

When Jack, Dale, and John decided to go with me rather than a less controversial company, I was actually doing well, but the media didn't know this or want to accept it quite yet. My company numbers were, especially from where I stood in the early nineties, quite astounding, but the press was still predicting my ultimate doom. There were other companies that could have been chosen and indeed were fighting hard for the contract, and they would have done a fine job. But none of the companies would have done the job that I did to develop the former Gulf + Western/Paramount building into what would become the most successful condominium tower ever to be built in the United States. GE, in the form of these three astute guys, knew that, but more important, they were willing to take the chance—one of the reasons GE is virtually in a class by itself.

It all began in 1994 when I started hearing stories that the GE pension fund had foreclosed on and was assuming control of the well-known fifty-two-story tower on Columbus Circle. Like all New Yorkers, I had known this building for many years. It stood at the corner of Central Park West and Central Park South, a unique location, and stuck out like a sore thumb because of its tremendous height relative to all other buildings along these two major New York City streets.

The Gulf + Western Building was erected in the early sixties just prior to the advent of a highly restrictive New York City zoning code that would greatly diminish the size and height of buildings constructed in that area. So this was a unique asset, a very tall tower that could never be built again in what would become one of the best locations anywhere.

The problem was that the tower had been erected by a New York City speculative builder as an office building and, unfortunately, was not built very well. Although the ceilings were very high throughout the building and the massing or shape of the building was absolutely fantastic—streamlined and classic—the outer curtain wall was cheap aluminum and glass, and in general the building was not well constructed. In addition, it swayed in the wind. Winds of only ten or fifteen miles an hour caused it to move or flex at the top, much more than buildings are supposed to.

This caused great anxiety within the building, even though, in actuality, it was very safe. The design was based on that of an airplane wing. The concept was that the winds would move the building much as an airplane wing moves or flaps, and that greater strength would be had for less money. It's a great idea—but not for a building. The concept goes down the drain when people live or work in the structure. You don't live in an airplane wing. You would hear stories that when the winds got high people were bailing out of the Gulf + Western Building, that the elevators would stop, and that some people would report feeling seasick. At the top, executive floors, occupied in its final years by a great executive named Marty Davis of Paramount Pictures, the movement was so great that company guests from the West Coast joked that they felt right at home—the building reminded them of California during an earthquake.

The building was a mess. Something had to be done about the flexible nature of the structure. And because the tower was constructed in the 1960s, it was totally laden with asbestos, which had to be removed.

Asbestos in itself has an interesting story. It is the greatest fireproofing material ever used, and everybody in the construction industry knows it. It is also 100 percent safe, once applied. But early on, asbestos got a bad rap because of the fact that miners who were digging asbestos for many years would often develop asbestosis, and therefore people thought that asbestos was not safe. I'm not saying it's the greatest material to work with. I'm only saying it's the safest material in terms of fire. A huge and concerted effort was made to have asbestos removed from buildings, causing tremendous dislocation and destruction and creating a new problem: asbestos floating in the air.

I believe that the movement against asbestos was led by the mob, because it was often mob-related companies that would do the asbestos removal. Great pressure was put on politicians, and as usual, the politicians relented. Millions of truckloads of this incredible fireproofing material were taken to special "dump sites," and asbestos was replaced by materials that were supposedly safe but couldn't hold a candle to asbestos in limiting the ravages of fire. In any event, because of this stupid law, we faced the huge task of removing the asbestos from every inch of steel in the building.

I'll never forget my first meeting with Dale Frey and John Myers, in 1994. I had heard that the building was for sale, and only knowing Dale Frey by reputation, I called him, introduced myself, and asked to meet. He was very receptive, although I later found out my call was only one of many. Every major developer in the country was calling him for the same reason. When I arrived at GE Investments in Stamford, Connecticut, John, Dale, and a group of their executives sat around a large conference table and listened to me go on and on about the fact that this building, which had to be virtually demolished and reconstructed anyway because of the asbestos and structural problems, should be remade into what could become one of the most successful residential developments in the country.

I told them that I expected the real estate market, especially the residential segment, to be getting very hot in the near future. I told them that even though the steel structure was a problem, the steel could be structuralized and strengthened, and that the reutilization of the steel would give very high ceilings and, most important, grandfathered zoning exceptions that could never be gotten again. If this steel were ripped down to the ground, a building of only nineteen stories, rather than the existing fifty-two, could be built in its place. This potentially spectacular structure with unparalleled views would garner the highest prices in New York, I said. I went on and on about the merits of this conversion, even stating that while an adequate office location, it actually was a much better residential location. Surprisingly, the building's long and rectangular shape didn't allow for very large office floors but was perfectly suited to superluxury apartments. After almost an hour, I shook hands with Dale and John and left, feeling like I'd really impressed them. Little did I realize how intrigued they actually were.

Most companies in their position would have taken their building, which they only got through adverse conditions in the first place, and sold it into what was then a very bad but improving real estate market. If they had done this, however, they would have received probably $25 million at most for this very troubled tower. Money was tight, and at that point in the New York cycle few banks would have been willing to spend approximately $250 million for a new residential development. Only a company with the imagination and strength of GE would have even thought of moving forward at that time.

GE was represented on this building by a fine man named Peter Ricker, president of the Galbreath Company. Peter is a real estate professional, and GE's choice couldn't have been better. In any event, Dale, John, and I would talk often by phone, and over a number of months I went back and forth to Stamford, showing my ideas in greater and greater detail to the GE folks. I knew they loved what I was saying but also knew that I had not yet emerged, in the eyes of the world, from the difficulties of the early 1990s. Perhaps GE, as a great institution, would be afraid to choose me over a "safer" alternative.

I will never forget in September of 1994 receiving a telephone call from Dale Frey. Dale is a very strong guy, but obviously this was a call he did not like making. "Donald," he said, "I think your ideas and your plans for the development of Trump International are very good, but I have no choice but to go out to bid. I've asked Peter Ricker and my staff to do a request for proposal to six or seven of the most prominent real estate firms in the country. I hope you'll bid on the project."

I couldn't believe it. I had worked so hard and my concept was so good, and now that I'd divulged all of my information, GE was going out to bid. I knew Dale had a fiduciary obligation to the pension fund, and I knew he took that obligation very seriously. But I still didn't understand why he couldn't just choose me. I said to him, "Dale, look, I think this is very unfair. I've worked very hard to come up with a plan that is truly spectacular, a plan that will work and make everybody a lot of money, especially GE. Why can't you just choose me and do away with this lengthy process of going to people that don't have my talent or imagination? I really felt that you liked me and my ideas. I don't understand what's going on."

"Look, Donald," Dale said, "I do like you and I do like your ideas, but I also have a very strong obligation to see what else is out there. I know that right now you don't feel like being one of the bidders, but I really want you to be. I think that with your talent and your ideas you really have a good chance of being chosen. Don't disappoint me and not bid."

I felt lousy. I even felt used. I had worked my ass off for months only to be told that I would be going into a bidding contest with top U.S. developers including Tishman-Speyer, Rouse, and others. I'd been in bidding contests before, and you never can tell what will happen. People come out of the woodwork and get chosen, often for all the wrong reasons. I didn't know what to do but ultimately persuaded myself, after receiving a huge package of information from GE regarding the bid, to go forward anyway. I felt like a schmuck, but what the hell did I have to lose at this point.

Weeks of preparation and study went into my bid. Magnificent renderings were drawn, architectural solutions were presented, along with sales plans showing numbers even the greatest optimist wouldn't believe. I had numerous meetings with Dale Frey, John Myers, Peter Ricker, and the GE staff, but nothing seemed to be happening. Time was going by, money was being spent, ideas were being put forward, but GE was playing its cards very close to the vest.

One of the best things I had in my favor was that GE's lawyer, one of the best in the business, was a man named Sandy Morhouse. Sandy and I had done many deals together in the early eighties, with Sandy always being on the other side. I didn't realize it at the time, but later I found out that Sandy was really pushing hard for me. His strong recommendation on my behalf would ultimately be very important.

In any event, I will not soon forget receiving a telephone call from Dale Frey. I was in a meeting in my office on a totally unrelated project, the possible expansion of the Trump Taj Mahal in Atlantic City, when word came to me that Dale wanted to see me as soon as possible. I called him to set up the appointment, and he said to me, "Donald, I would like to see you at your earliest convenience—I think you'll be very happy with my news." I knew immediately what that meant and was extremely happy. The deal that I had proposed to GE had been chosen over all others, and a joint-venture partnership would be formed. I told Dale that I really appreciated his choice and that he would not be sorry. This would be not only a very profitable venture, but also one where he would have a great deal of fun. Little did I realize at the time just how profitable, and how much fun we would all have. Demolition of the Gulf + Western tower, everything but the steel, began in April of 1995.

GE always had problems with the idea of going into the construction business in New York, but I assured them that the best builders and workers anywhere in the world are, in fact, located right here in New York City. They soon began to see this for themselves. The building came down like magic, with four or five stories a week of curtain wall being removed and demolition of everything inside moving at a pace far beyond anyone's expectation but mine.

Even people throughout New York City, because of the huge view exposure of this building, were astounded at how fast the steel frame seemed to be uncovered. They watched the transformation of a building before their eyes in a period most people felt was impossible, about twelve months. The plan was devised to build 264 superluxury residential units, 164 hotel suites, and a magnificent restaurant at the base. There would also be parking and a world-class health spa with a swimming pool. Decisions were made at meetings with GE, Peter Ricker, Dan Galbreath, Bruce Warwick, Scott Coopcheck, and my incredible staff led by construction wizard Andy Weiss and Charlie Reiss, an expert on the municipal-approval process.

Many decisions were made during this time, always with quality in mind. The highest-grade marbles were used, the best bathroom and kitchen fixtures were chosen, and in all instances, from everybody's point of view, this building was conceived and dedicated to the proposition of simply being "the best." Various designs for the restructuralization and strengthening of the steel frame were presented, and we chose the most expensive and most effective one. Essentially, we would be building two huge sheer walls right through the middle of the building, in the form of a cross, starting from the foundation and rising almost to the top. These walls, made of concrete and steel, would be totally rigid to prevent the building from moving. Construction went well, but sales went even better. From the instant our prospectus was approved by the New York State Attorney General's Office, the apartments sold rapidly.

I set up a sales office at Trump Parc, another nearby building I built. The sales office was staffed by Louise Sunshine and Judy Ban-

*Trump International, while under construction, as viewed
from the rooftop of the Carnegie Mews Building.*

ham of the Sunshine Group and featured a special movie theater
showing a seven-minute video on New York and the building itself.

Little did I realize just how much homework GE had done. Prior
to choosing me, GE had spent a great deal of time, effort, and money
on asking the outside brokerage and consulting world what effect the
name Trump would have on the success of the building. When the
results came in, it was determined that not only would the Trump

Trump International—The Beginning: November 1995.

name add perhaps as much as $200 a foot (it later turned out to be much more than that), but more important to GE, the building would sell at a much faster pace than it would have otherwise. I was never made totally privy to the final results, but I heard that the numbers were staggering, and in the end this, coupled with the strong recommendation of Sandy Morhouse and others in the industry, was the main reason for having chosen me.

A big decision yet to be made was what we would do with the restaurant. It was always wonderful to have a great restaurant, but great restaurants are hard to make. There were different camps and different choices. Every restaurant company wanted to be associated with this project, and the space was very easy to rent, but much more important than the rent were the quality and reputation of who we would put in. Many top restaurants were looked at, some with big reputations and bad service, others with big names, who would pay big rents but who would not give the building the kind of prestige I wanted.

Prestige was very important to me on this project, and that's one of the reasons that I wanted, very much, to use Philip Johnson as the architect. Philip's name, in conjunction with Costas, Kondylis Associates, added a great deal of class, and I certainly did not want to lose that with probably our most important decision, food and food ser-

Trump International—Work in Progress: December 1995

vice. We interviewed David Bouley and almost made a deal with him, but in the end he asked for many changes that would have been unacceptable to me and the others. We spoke to Victor Dray, one of the top restaurateurs in California, but even though he would have been a good choice we just weren't sure whether or not his heart was into moving to New York. In the end, the decision was not even a close one. Jean-Georges Vongerichten is considered the best chef in the United States by almost everyone. Luckily for us, he wanted to open a new restaurant, and luckily for him, we had the space. We could have gotten much more rent than Jean Georges would be paying from almost anyone else, but it was our decision to seek the best restaurant anywhere—and what a decision it was. The restaurant, Jean Georges, opened to the finest reviews given in literally decades. Almost all the restaurant critics rated Jean Georges four stars.

Time passed, with no review yet from the highly respected food critic of *The New York Times,* Ruth Reichl. But then one day it hit: a great review for Jean Georges—four stars all the way:

> On the surface, Jean Georges looks like just another expensive new restaurant. It is tempting to abandon yourself to the sensual pleasure of the place, sink into the comfortable seats and allow the staff to surround you with aroma and seduce you with flavor. But take a deeper look: in his quiet way the chef and co-owner, Jean-Georges Vongerichten, is creating a restaurant revolution. This is an entirely new kind of four-star restaurant. . . . If a walk in the woods were translated to flavor, it would be his porcini tart, a rich pastry spread with a deeply flavored walnut-and-onion paste and topped with sauteed mushrooms. The salad served on the side, a mixture of wild leaves (chickweed, plantain, sheep's sorrel, and dandelion), heightens the impression. . . . The flavors are astonishing . . . but there is more. In the end, Mr. Vongerichten is a romantic. Before he sends you out the door, he showers you with chocolate, macaroons, homemade marshmallows, and candied rose petals.

Trump International—Restoration Complete.

This turned out to be one of our really great decisions. There are only four four-star restaurants in New York, and we had one of them. Not only that, but this is the first time in memory that a new restaurant has received four stars from *The New York Times.* Our biggest problem with Jean Georges is that there is a six-month waiting list to get in. The phones in my office are continually ringing with friends and enemies alike asking me to help them get a reservation. This is definitely a problem I do not mind having.

Hey, I enjoy good company! It's not bad to hang out with the most beautiful women in the world!

MASTER OF THE UNIVERSE:

HOW I GOT THE BEAUTY PAGEANT

I HATE TRAFFIC. I HATE ANYTHING THAT SLOWS ME DOWN. Takeoff was scheduled for 3:00 P.M., which at the time seemed plausible, except that the traffic to the airport was insane. Luckily, it was my plane we were heading to, my plane, so it's not as if I could have missed the flight. But I had several meetings awaiting me in Miami and countless details to straighten out before the pageant. Finally, the traffic thinned out along the Long Island Expressway. We arrived at 3:15 P.M.—not bad.

Certain aspects of my work are grueling. Witness the Riverside South project: Years of meetings, protests, impact studies, petulant West Side neighbors, lawsuits, and, after a decade of battles—victory. Other aspects of my work, though, are much more pleasant. I like to mix it up. That way I never stop having fun. Witness the Miss Universe contest. The battle to buy it wasn't a cinch, but basically, Miss Universe isn't about laborious, bureaucratic madness, like Riverside South, it's about fun; and it's about beauty, the ultimate beauty—that of a woman.

Our four limos pulled up next to the jet black 727, a giant red *T* inscribed on the tail. I stepped onto the tarmac. Eva Herzigova, one of the most beautiful models in the world, stepped out after me. My assistant on the book was behind her, carrying a tiny laptop computer the size of a dictionary. Eva's husband, Tico, the drummer for Bon Jovi, stepped out next. Terry Botwick, my partner from CBS, followed—he had a laptop, too—along with an entourage of friends, employees, and bodyguards. We clambered into the plane and sat down. I called toward the cockpit: "Wheels up!"

Everyone settled in for the two-hour flight. Eva had just rolled off the Concorde after cat-walking the fashion shows in Paris and Milan. I glanced up at her. With no makeup, her hair uncombed, clothes thrown on, she was still one of the most beautiful women I have ever seen. It's a whole different category of beauty.

Her husband was charming. We were sitting across from each other, and he proclaimed out of the blue: "Hey, Donald, dude, you should get yourself a haircut."

I never thought I'd become the owner of the Miss Universe Pageant, but I certainly welcomed the chance to buy it. Along with Miss Universe came Miss USA and Miss Teen USA, affectionately known as the triple crown of beauty. I first saw the Miss Universe

You wouldn't believe the gas this baby guzzles.

Pageant live in 1996, when I attended the broadcast from Las Vegas. Marla hosted the show along with Bob Goen, the handsome co-anchor of *Entertainment Tonight.* Because of Marla's involvement, I arrived in Las Vegas early and toured the workings of the event, both backstage and front. It was during this time that I heard rumblings that Miss Universe might be sold by its owner, Madison Square Garden Corporation. MSG was owned by ITT, which was looking to pare down assets. Miss Universe didn't quite fit in with the very sports-minded people at Madison Square Garden (although I'm sure the Knicks and Rangers players could have been beautifully inspired by this asset).

After hearing these rumors, I decided to call Joe Cohen, a talented friend of mine, who also happened to graduate in my class at the Wharton School of Finance. Over the years, Joe had had a series of entertainment and sports successes and had risen to the presidency of the Madison Square Garden Television Network. Joe explained to me that the Garden would, indeed, be selling Miss Universe, Miss USA, and Miss Teen USA and that he thought it would be a great acquisition for me. In fact, after I bought it, Cindy Adams, a good friend and a society columnist for the *New York Post*, wrote the following piece:

Donald Trump, Master of the Universe?

Let me tell you the history of Mr. Terrific's fascination with the Miss Universe Pageant.

Way back when we first met, back before the earth cooled, back before Trump Tower, Trump Plaza, Trump Parc, Trump Castle, Trump Palace, Trump Taj, Trump Ivana, Trump Marla, Trump Air, Trump Princess, Trump helicopters, Trump everything, back when Trump was just a bridge term, he was just a young whiz fresh out of Wharton and I was Assistant to the President of the Miss Universe Pageant.

We're talking 1971. The mother of all beauty pageants was then owned by hosiery company Kayser-Roth. Until me, it had been for years out of California and Miami. I'm the one who made the international Miss Universe Pageant international. I put it in Greece, I called Imelda Marcos and put it in the Philippines, I made the deal for it to beam out of Hong Kong. I also booked the celebrity judges.

At a dinner party, lawyer Roy Cohn had introduced Donald to me with: "This guy will own New York someday." I said, "Yeah, yeah, pass the gravy." Who knew he'd own the world someday? His dinner partner that night was, as always, a drop-dead gorgeous blonde. With a neckline so low she probably still has bronchitis. And brainy? Couldn't spell CIA. He and I kept talking across Blondie's puffy chest. We laughed all night. We loved one another instantly.

Come July. Miss Universe time. I'd organized a parade of contestants in hansom cabs down Broadway. Cops studded the route. Nobody was allowed near the contestants in the line of march. I look over. Who's alongside some nifty beauty from some Who-Knows-Where-Country? My brand-new Best Friend. He wasn't The Donald then. Yet he was the only one who'd broken the line and was walking right with them.

That night I invited certain people to a Miss Universe party. Among them U.N. Ambassador George Bush and my pal Donny. After dinner the girls were sequestered in a hotel. Chaperoned, yet. Guess who somehow, somewhere, someplace ended up personally improving international relations? The pre-Ivana Donald Trump.

I couldn't know then that he'd turn out to be a financial and marketing genius, but I did know then that nothing could stop him. Nothing he couldn't accomplish. I also knew then that he loved beauty, loved blondes, and loved the Miss Universe Pageant.

I guess it's safe to say that Cindy Adams predicted it, my recent acquisition, as she has predicted a series of events in my life. I'd love to borrow her crystal ball!

So Miss Universe was up for sale, and I was intrigued. How could I pass up the opportunity to own the world's premiere beauty pageant? Of course, there were more than twenty other parties wanting it also, proving that where there is glamour and beauty, there will always be people with money wanting to get in on the act. And what could be more beautiful or more glamorous than this?

I started negotiating in earnest with Madison Square Garden. Soon I received several strange phone calls from one of my lawyers at the time, Bert Fields, a prominent West Coast entertainment attorney. Knowing of my interest in acquiring the pageant, he asked that I meet with Gustavo Cisneros, a man I knew by reputation only as one of the wealthiest men in South America, who also happened to own the Miss Venezuela pageant. In Venezuela, as in most South American countries, beauty pageants are a national obsession. On the day of the pageant, the entire country shuts down.

Bert Fields kept bugging me, telling me that Gustavo Cisneros also wanted to buy the pageant. He asked if I would meet with Cisneros. Why? I asked. Why would I want to meet with a competing bidder, unless he was considering a partnership?

Bert wasn't sure, or at least so he told me, why Cisneros kept insisting on a meeting. But after rejecting his advances initially, I reluctantly agreed to meet. After all, Bert was my lawyer, and I assumed he had my best interests at heart. Bert was later to insist that he told me Cisneros was his client. I don't remember it that way.

Cisneros invited me to his apartment, an absolutely magnificent blocklong duplex on Fifth Avenue. He couldn't have been more of a gentleman. There I stood beneath twenty-foot ceilings, the walls lined with Italian Masters worth millions. It was a beautiful place, all top of the line. Gustavo himself was dazzlingly handsome, a distinguished European aristocrat with slicked-back hair and a swarthy complexion. I had on a suit; he wore a beautiful burgundy silk robe. I thought at the time that if I were casting a movie whose male lead was to be South American aristocracy, the role would go to him. He was truly elegant. Breakfast was a production, with several butlers—all dressed in white, all elegant—waiting on us. The service was impeccable. I learned something about style that morning.

We sat down in his living room and discussed everything *but* the Miss Universe contest. This said to me that Cisneros wanted it. Bert Fields was present also, having flown in from L.A. Finally, as we finished breakfast, Cisneros popped the question.

"Are you looking to buy Miss Universe?" he said.

"Why do you ask?" I replied.

"For many, many years I've wanted to buy it, and this seems to be my opportunity."

I admitted that I was interested in acquiring the pageant. Then, to my astonishment, he asked me what price I would pay.

"Why do you ask me that, Gustavo?" I said. "Do you want to be my partner?"

He insisted in his staccato Spanish accent, "No, I don't want you as my partner. I don't want anyone as my partner. But what price are you going to pay?"

I sat there thinking to myself, Does he think all Americans are stupid?

He continued to press. I thought about it for a while, and I realized this was the most ridiculous business negotiation—if you want to call it that—I'd ever had. I glared at Bert. There he sat across the table from me, also a rather elegant-looking guy, and I asked him with my eyes, "How the hell did you put me into this situation? You knew I didn't want to be here, so why did you keep pushing for this meeting?"

That's when I decided to have some fun. This was the most unprofessional encounter I'd had in a long time. There was no way I could wander outside the bounds of reason.

"Gustavo," I said, "I'd love to do the entire deal for about four million." Notice the language—*love to,* not *intend to.* "I doubt they would do it for that, but if they ever did, I would certainly be interested." What I didn't tell him was that I would also be interested at a much higher price. Surprisingly, he didn't question me further.

In a very unusual gesture, at least for Americans, Gustavo walked me to the elevator, descended with me to the lobby, and walked me outside to my waiting car. He then looked at me and simply said, "Good-bye, and thank you, Donald."

Bert remained behind in the apartment as I thought to myself what a strange meeting this was. Why would anybody be asked to state the price he intended to pay for a competitively bid asset, especially to another bidder? This was a classic!

Less than three hours later the guys from ITT/Madison Square Garden arrived at my office. We cut a deal for $10 million—that was surprising, because they had been asking for much more.

"HONEY, I'M HOME!!"

1996 Copyright, NYP Holdings, Inc. Reprinted with permission from the New York Post.

I called Gustavo the following morning.

"Donald, Donald, Donald, how are you?"

"I'm fine, Gustavo. I wanted you to hear it from me, the horse's mouth. I just bought the Miss Universe contest."

He went ballistic. "No! No! No! This is not possible."

"Yes, Gustavo, I just bought the Miss Universe pageant."

"How much did you pay?" he screamed.

"Ten million."

"You told me you were going to pay four million," he barked.

"No, Gustavo, I didn't tell you I was going to pay four million. I told you I would *love* to pay four million, not that I *intended* to bid four million."

"This is terrible," he moaned. "This is terrible."

"Gustavo, look," I said. "You didn't want to do a partnership. Why would I tell you what I would pay? There was no reason for me to do so. I had no obligation to tell you what I was prepared to pay. And I still can't believe that you would ask me, assuming that we weren't going to be partners."

Life is not all bad!

All he could do was continue to repeat, seemingly in a trance, "This is just terrible, this is just terrible." Then he hung up. You've got to understand that this was not a victory call, a kind of rub-it-in-your-face call. I'm polite. It was a courtesy call. I didn't want him to hear it from anyone else.

Then, much to my surprise, Bert Fields called. That was a big mistake. If he'd given me a few days to cool down, I might not have bawled him out. Not only did he disturb me, but he had the audacity to imply that I had deceived his client. I blew up and told him he never should have set up the meeting in the first place. Then I fired him. (He says he quit.)

I'm a lot better off without Bert Fields anyway. I think he's highly overrated, and his high legal fees were a continuing source of irritation to me. I continued to use the firm but not Fields. In retrospect, Gustavo Cisneros did me a big favor.

Lawyers in general really bother me. For instance, often a case will be presented to me in which I am being sued for X dollars and a settlement will be offered for substantially less than what my legal fees would be. Depending on the type of case it is, I will often reject the settlement. When a businessman becomes known as someone who easily settles cases, it creates a very bad precedent. While it may often be the thing to do, it allows vulture lawyers to watch various companies and see who are and who aren't the "settlers." The moment someone settles or makes it easy for a particular lawyer, he will inevitably return with another suit a short time later. Also, his scavenger friends who were watching will likewise find reason to sue.

Litigation in the United States has gotten totally out of control. It has actually become an accepted business practice for people to use the court's time, money, and energy in order to effect deals, break up deals, and receive money unjustly. I know people who virtually can't function without starting a lawsuit, thinking that this will give them the upper hand in even the most simple of negotiations.

Politicians ought to be ashamed of themselves for perpetuating this ridiculous situation. Court systems have become backlogged for years with superfluous cases. In New York in particular, a case will often take seven or eight years to actually get to court. This is certainly not the judge's fault, because most of the judges in New York are hard-working, diligent men and women with brilliant legal minds. The fault lies in a system that is meant to be abused, and which is costing states and the country hundreds of millions of dollars. Perhaps more important, it's creating centuries' worth of delay. The saddest part of all is that this problem should be easy to solve, and everybody, including the American Bar Association, knows exactly what I'm talking about. The simple answer is this: *The loser pays all costs related to the case including, but in no way limited to, the legal fees of the winning party.*

If this legislation were enacted, it is my opinion that you would see our courthouses become totally efficient again, in that the case-load would drop by perhaps 70 to 80 percent. The judges and their staffs, who now work endlessly to catch up with needless motions made by nonsense lawyers, would be free to concentrate on the real cases, the ones that deserve to go to court. Everyone knows I'm right, but no politician wants to take on the wrath of the lawyers' lobbying groups. Somebody should—because that person could be assured of being in office forever.

Lawyers, and their billing in particular, have gotten out of hand in this country. Often you will be involved in what you think is a very simple and straightforward deal with normal legal work, and you end up with a legal fee that would choke a horse. You believe the lawyers you are dealing with are honest, yet in your own mind there is just no way you can justify to yourself paying the bill. Over the last number of years I've been slapped with many legal fees that were downright dishonest. Attorneys were often doing totally unnecessary work and then taking longer to do it so there would be more hours to bill. Bills are customarily inflated and often claim fees for more people than are even available in the office.

Once a major New York law firm that did a considerable amount of work for me sent in bills of more than $5 million within a two- or three-year period. After careful study and investigation, I discovered that much of their billing was incorrect. I threatened major litigation against the firm. Needless to say, the $5 million bill was reviewed by the firm and quickly reduced to the more realistic fee of $200,000. Some people would say this is great negotiation. I would say it's a total disgrace to the legal profession.

After negotiating with ITT/Madison Square Garden, I was pleasantly surprised to hear that CBS wanted Miss Universe, too. So CBS liked the product, and CBS liked me. I, likewise, liked CBS. I've always had tremendous respect for Les Moonves, who I knew something about prior to the purchase. Recognizing a great opportunity, I offered to go partners.

Having a broadcaster as my partner was a terrific strategic advantage. No other bidder had guaranteed television viewing. The other bidders were scared and their bids were low.

The pageant in Miami Beach, my first as owner, was a huge success. We'd sold out the house; it was a mob scene. From my position offstage, I was able to glance up to the greenroom occasionally. I could just see Alicia Machado, the current Miss Universe, sitting there plumply. God, what problems I had with this woman. First, she wins. Second, she gains fifty pounds. Third, I urge the committee *not* to fire her. Fourth, I go to the gym *with* her, in a show of support. Final act: She trashes me in *The Washington Post*—after I stood by her the entire time. What's wrong with this picture? Anyway, the best part about the evening was the knowledge that next year, she would no longer be Miss Universe.

What's maddening is that I supported her. Even in Palm Beach, where I haven't always gotten the greatest press, Shannon Donnelly, society columnist for the Palm Beach *Daily News,* wrote, "Here's a new one for The Donald: Protector-Advocate for large women. His acquisition from ITT has put Alicia Machado under the Trump Aegis. The Donald, bless his heart, doesn't want to fire her because 'it would be a terrible message to send.' He is instead bringing her to the spa at Mar-a-Lago where she can work out in earnest, eat sensibly and generally decompress." That sounds pretty gentlike to me.

Anyway, the pageant was finally winding down, and the last three contestants—Miss Trinidad-Tobago, Miss Venezuela, and Miss USA—were about to hear the final question. George Hamilton, our emcee, put two of the three women in soundproof glass cylinders so they wouldn't be able to hear the question. Hamilton queried Miss Venezuela, "If you could do anything—something crazy and completely out of character—what would you do?"

She is a total beauty, but she blew it. She said something ludicrous about traveling around the world, to Israel, all in one day; most of it was inaudible. In all fairness to her, though, I don't think she understood the question. Some of these women deal with an interpreter.

Next came Miss USA, from Hawaii, a dark horse with a brilliant personality who charged from behind to win Miss USA. She answered well under pressure. She is really pretty and cute, with a great big smile and a great body, too. Her answer came quickly and naturally. Miss USA walked downstage and answered, with that wide smile: "I would eat everything in sight! I would eat it all." At that point she patted her perfectly toned stomach. "And I would eat it all twice!" The audience went nuts. I knew then that she was the winner.

Marla looked beautiful. She's so good at this kind of stuff. I guess her hosting the contest was a testament to her ability to handle pressure.

Not to my surprise, almost at the top of the show, George Hamilton said to Marla, "You look like you've lost a little weight."

She smiled that million-dollar smile. "Yes, George," she said in her southern drawl. "About two hundred pounds."

The cameras all beamed on me, and everyone in the audience and, I assume, everyone watching on television, thought I was very angry. Actually, this exchange was written into the script, and approved by me prior to the contest. But it played well and actually took some of the heat off a very hot situation—Marla and I had announced we were splitting up just about a week before the show aired. The announcement ran wild as a front-page story all over the place. Some people actually suggested that I staged the timing in order to get high ratings on the Miss Universe contest. Nothing could be further from the truth. As the stories about this were written, I said to myself, "What kind of a mind could even imagine doing this?"

The pageant was a hit, receiving an 18 share, the highest-rated 9:00 P.M. Friday-night show on CBS in four years. The party afterward was fun, but I had had enough. It was time to go. As I walked out the back, I saw the pageant president, Maureen Reidy, gabbing with some of her assistants. "Let's go, girls." I said. We all climbed into the back of a limo. I heard the buzz of motorcycles—Harleys. I suddenly looked up and saw no fewer than six Miami police officers on Harley-Davidsons surrounding the limo—it was a veritable motorcade. What a way to arrive at the hotel. What a scene. It was a blast. You see, I can have fun, too. It's all part of the formula.

LECLARE ASSOCIATES

Trump Tower: My old and loyal friend.

TRUMP TOWER:

OLD FAITHFUL

IT WOULD BE VERY HARD FOR ME TO WRITE A BOOK ABOUT coming back without at least a brief mention of my favorite building, Trump Tower, located on Fifth Avenue and Fifty-seventh Street. Readers of my first book know the details about Trump Tower—when it was built, its size, and what it represents. It has become a true icon in New York, a place that draws record numbers of tourists and visitors. Adding the tremendous allure of the new NIKETOWN store on Fifty-seventh Street, a major part of the atrium, I would venture to say that Trump Tower draws the biggest crowds in New York City. More important than that, however, is that Trump Tower, like a good friend, was there when I needed it.

During the hard times of the early 1990s, cash flow was tight for most real estate developers. Most buildings were a disaster, with great amounts of empty space and lots of ugly flowing red ink. But even in the worst of times, Trump Tower, together with the huge cash flows of my casinos, was there for me. I'll never forget the time, in the worst moment of the real estate crisis, when I was notified that a major retail tenant, Charles Jourdan, was experiencing great difficulty worldwide and would not be able to stay as a tenant in Trump Tower any longer.

Charles Jourdan was once a great shoe store, but you could see by what was happening at its Fifth Avenue store that things were not good. Their racks looked cheap, and the displays were horrible. I can walk into a retail establishment and, just by looking at it, tell you how it's doing. With Charles Jourdan, it became obvious.

Unfortunately, Charles Jourdan was paying a very high rent for its large Fifth Avenue–fronting store. When I heard that these millions of dollars in rental income and taxes would be lost, I said to somebody, "This is really bad news. How will I ever replace this one?" But as bad as times were, when the word got out that this store was available, I was inundated with rental requests. Many prestigious stores were calling me either directly or through some high contact; even top politicians and celebrities were contacting me with recommendations as to who should occupy the space.

I soon began to realize that even in the worst of times something great will always be great. After assessing all bids, and not merely for the dollars paid, I decided on Salvatore Ferragamo because of its fine reputation and incredible success. They have since built a tremendous store, are doing fabulous business, and the rental that I lost was, after the fact, insignificant. Trump Tower had come through again.

A similar story happened with Nike. A major portion of the atrium, fronting on Fifty-seventh Street, was occupied originally by Bonwit Teller, then the French store Galeries Lafayette. The French representatives of Galeries were extremely arrogant, and it was not long after they rented the store that I realized this would not be a very successful tenant. They took the very beautiful Bonwit Teller space and, rather than fixing it up and quickly opening a new store, decided to do a massive construction job. This, in and of itself, was good—until I saw what they were doing.

They stripped the store virtually down to its steel frame to build an almost identical new store, but with lower ceilings, fluorescent lighting, and cheap flooring to replace the marble that had existed before. They spent tens of millions of dollars, wasted over a year in construction, and in the end destroyed what could have been a magnificent space for a fraction of the cost. I then saw their advertising campaign and listened as their people proudly announced that Galeries Lafayette would be using designers that I had never even heard of—not a good sign! At first I figured that they must know what they were doing, but I quickly realized they were playing right into the hands of Bergdorf Goodman, Saks Fifth Avenue, and all of the other great retailers who had stores in that part of town. People don't want to hear about second tier, especially at Fifth Avenue and Fifty-seventh Street.

Needless to say, they did terribly right from the start, which is not easy to do at probably the best retail location in the world. After a couple of years of astronomical losses, the top representative of Galeries Lafayette came to my office and, in a very severe French accent, said to me, "We will be leaving this space, whether you like it or not."

I looked at him and said, "Unfortunately, you have a lease. You won't be leaving so quickly or certainly without a major payment."

Galeries Lafayette was paying a rent of $3 million a year, which I didn't want to lose in the early 1990s. I also knew, however, that this store would never make it, and other than the rent, I was not particularly thrilled about them being in Trump Tower. What I really didn't like, however, was the attitude of the top people telling me that they were leaving whether I liked it or not, when in fact they had a very strong legal obligation to me. I looked the Galeries rep in the eye again and said, "Listen, I'll let you out of your lease, but you have to pay me fifty million dollars."

I knew from reading *Women's Wear Daily* and other trade publications that they were losing tremendous amounts of money in this store—some estimates were as high as $18 million and more. If you were losing $18 million a year, what does $50 million really mean? It's less than three years of losses, and there were eleven or twelve years left on the lease. He looked at me with great scorn and told me that he would never pay to get out of his lease. But I knew he would. The following week he came back to see me and offered a package that amounted to many millions. I almost fell out of my chair.

It was the last thing I ever thought I would see at the world's best location—a tenant paying that much money to terminate its lease. We worked out the deal, but even prior to working it out I wanted to see what my options were and I began looking for new tenants. What materialized was really amazing. NIKETOWN had been looking for years for a great showplace, a museum of what has become probably the hottest brand in the world.

They could never build what they envisioned in any other city, but New York was special, and they decided to go forward and make me an offer I couldn't refuse. The rent was far greater than what I was getting from Galeries Lafayette. And on top of that, they wanted to rip down the entire store, which didn't really fit their needs, and build

One of the great buildings of the world!

a new Nike megastore. The money and genius that they poured into this store was staggering, but the end product is total justification. It has turned out to be one of the most successful stores in New York. And I have a wonderful tenant paying lots and lots of rent. Again, Trump Tower came through for me.

From the very beginning the stores and offices in Trump Tower have been successful in every way and certainly beyond even my wildest expectations. The apartments in this sixty-eight-story building are occupied by some of the greatest names in the world and sell for amounts that are out of this world. While the casinos are bigger and throw off far more cash, it's always been really nice to have my friend, Trump Tower, chugging along and hitting home run after home run. Every time someone leaves Trump Tower, they are replaced with a better tenant paying more rent. And the beauty of it all is that there is no doubt in my mind this trend will continue for the foreseeable future, despite economic conditions. Some things are so good that times don't affect them. Trump Tower is one of those things.

Marla and me in happier times.

THE WOMEN IN
(AND OUT) OF MY LIFE

PART OF THE PROBLEM I'VE HAD WITH WOMEN HAS BEEN IN having to compare them to my incredible mother, Mary Trump. My mother is smart as hell. I remember once, a long time ago, my sister Maryanne, a highly respected federal judge in New Jersey, told me that my mother is one of the smartest people she ever met. At the time it didn't make much of an impact on me, and I didn't really understand why she said it. All I knew was that my mother was a really great homemaker and wife to my father, Fred—a wonderful guy but not the easiest person to be married to.

But now I fully understand why Maryanne made that statement, and it is 100 percent true. In a soft and beautiful way, my mother has always been able to make an impact. As a younger woman she was a great beauty, but her inner beauty was even greater. I got very lucky in having Fred and Mary as parents. I could not have done any better.

I grew up in a very normal family. I was always of the opinion that aggression, sex drive, and everything that goes along with it was on the man's part of the table, not the woman's. As I grew older and witnessed life firsthand from a front-row seat at the great clubs, social events, and parties of the world—I have seen just about everything—I began to realize that women are far stronger than men. Their sex drive makes us look like babies. Some women try to portray themselves as being of the weaker sex, but don't believe it for a minute.

If I told the real stories of my experiences with women, often seemingly very happily married and important women, this book would be a guaranteed best-seller (which it will be anyway!). I'd love to tell all, using names and places, but I just don't think it's right. Now, I respect Geraldo Rivera. Nobody covered the O. J. Simpson case with more verve or flair than Geraldo, and I really like him very much. I have been on his show, and he is a total professional. But when he wrote a book describing his sexual conquests in great detail, using names and places, I really disapproved, and I would be willing to bet that if Geraldo had it to do over again, he would not have named names. What happens in the bedroom is very private and is not supposed to be exposed by either partner. But Geraldo is right in that lots of things do happen, things that are very surprising and things with women whom you would least suspect.

I remember attending a magnificent dinner being given by one of the most admired people in the world. I was seated next to a lady of great social pedigree and wealth. Her husband was sitting on the other side of the table, and we were having a very nice but extremely straight conversation. All of a sudden I felt her hand on my knee, then on my leg. She started petting me in all different ways. I looked at her and asked, "Is everything all right?" I didn't want to make a scene in a ballroom full of five hundred VIPs. The amazing part about her was who she was—one of the biggest of the big. She then asked me to dance, and I accepted. While we were dancing she became very aggressive, and I said, "Look, we have a problem. Your husband is sitting at that table, and so is my wife."

"Donald," she said, "I don't care. I just don't care. I have to have you, and I have to have you now." I told her that I'd call her, but she had to stop the behavior immediately. She made me promise, and I did. When I called I just called to say hello, and that was the end of that.

But the level of aggression was unbelievable. This is not infrequent, it happens all the time. One woman, who was also socially prominent, was getting married, and I had bumped into her on Fifth Avenue while she was exchanging wedding gifts. I had my limousine nearby, and she asked if I could give her a ride back to her apartment on Park Avenue. I said absolutely, not even suspecting that within five seconds after the door closed she would be jumping on top of me wanting to get screwed. I said, "You're getting married next week, and I'm going to your wedding."

"I don't really care," she said. "I never liked him that much anyway, and you know that." I was really in a quandary, because she is a truly great-looking and sexy woman.

Women have one of the great acts of all time. The smart ones act very feminine and needy, but inside they are real killers. The person who came up with the expression "the weaker sex" was either very naïve or had to be kidding. I have seen women manipulate men with just a twitch of their eye—or perhaps another body part. I have seen some of the roughest, toughest guys on earth, guys who rant and rave at other tough guys and make them cry, and yet they're afraid of their 120-pound girlfriends or wives. I know a man who makes mincemeat out of almost any man he looks at. When he walks through the city, people cross to the other side of the street. He is afraid of no one, and became very wealthy and very powerful with this attitude. But when his five-foot-two wife calls him and screams at him that he's always late for dinner and it better not happen again, he rushes out of the office without a moment's hesitation, shouting, "Donny, I have to go, she's going to kill me. I swear she's going to kill me."

There's nothing I love more than women, but they're really a lot different than portrayed. They are far worse than men, far more aggressive, and boy, can they be smart. Let's give credit where credit is due, and let's salute women for their tremendous power, which most men are afraid to admit they have.

Most people think they have me figured out—a single-minded businessman, an infallible negotiator. Others see me as someone devoted to beauty, to performance. The truth is, I am both of these people. Witness the difference between the two women who have meant the most to me in my life to date, Ivana and Marla. Both are incredibly talented and successful women in their own right. And, sure, they're both blond and beautiful. But they are completely different from each other. Ivana is a tough and practical businesswoman; Marla is a performer and actress. Over the past year, I have come to realize that these two exceptional women represent the extremes of my personality. The impact they've had on me is profound.

In the fall of 1989 I was flying back from Tokyo after witnessing the greatest upset in the history of professional boxing—the defeat of Iron Mike Tyson at the hands of Buster Douglas, a virtual unknown. We were about an hour shy of landing in Alaska for refueling when my airplane phones started ringing off the hooks. Apparently, while I was away, Ivana had told Liz Smith, the widely read New York gossip columnist, that our marriage was breaking up. The story appeared on the front page of the *Sunday Daily News,* which at the time had the largest circulation in the country. When I landed in New York, I discovered that media interest in me and Ivana was greater than I ever could have imagined. For weeks we were in the headlines of newspapers all over the world. Not since the divorce of Elizabeth Taylor and Richard Burton had there been such media hoopla.

It had been my idea to get a divorce, and since everything had already been set into motion by Ivana, I knew that the inevitable breakup of our marriage could no longer be denied. Even though I liked and loved Ivana a lot and she loved me, people grow apart. I'll never say a bad thing about her, but sometimes you have to make a decision: Do you stay or do you go? To me it was obvious; I didn't go home that night but instead took a suite at the Plaza Hotel. This meant that there was no way I could win the inevitable PR war, at least for the time being, so I just sat back and let it happen. Ivana, on the other hand, hired John Scanlon, a PR man, who only added fuel to the fire. It didn't take long for Ivana's publicity machine to take advantage of the media tide in her favor; when a man leaves a woman, the public relations war is impossible for him to win. As our settlement proceedings approached, Scanlon began to focus less on her claims that she had been emotionally devastated by the separation and more on the financial aspects of the case. Since, according to Ivana, I had assets totaling $5 billion, Ivana's lawyers asserted that the $25 million provided for her upon our divorce in the 1987 prenuptial agreement she had signed was too small a share. There was little I could do except wait for her lawyers to slap me with a lawsuit that laid claim to half of every piece of property in my possession at the time.

During this period, it came to my attention that there are people who believe I am incapable of having bad financial times. It is their theory that I purposely set out to create a financially bad period in order to quickly settle my divorce. This theory was further fueled in their minds by the coincidence that things started going well for me almost immediately after Ivana agreed to settle. They felt that everything I did had a purpose. They could not have been more wrong.

Ivana hired Michael Kennedy to be her lead counsel. He was assisted by the prestigious law firm of White & Case. For some time, I had known of Kennedy as someone who defended people accused of narcotics offenses. He also defended the Mitchell brothers, the porn-movie kings who produced *Behind the Green Door*. When Ivana took him on, he managed to get himself a profile in *The New York Times*. Suddenly he was heralded as the man who would champion women's rights.

Meanwhile, I had to find my own legal team. My office resembled an emergency room, but instead of patients, there were lawyers, crowding around and offering their services. Some were so eager to become involved in what promised to become one of the most publicized and talked-about divorces in the past twenty-five years that they assured me there would be no legal fees. I interviewed many of these people, but no one satisfied me. I was looking for a special kind of attorney—one who had not only great ability but also a deep sense of loyalty to me and my interests. I would not be stripped of the great empire I had worked so hard to build.

Finally, on a Wednesday morning in February—Valentine's Day to be exact—I received a phone call from Edward S. Gordon, a major real estate executive in New York. Gordon is a friend as well as a business associate, and I had really come to respect his opinion. He said, "Donald, do I have a quinella for you!" (He used gambling parlance to mean he had a combination he believed would serve my interests.) He told me about Stanford Lotwin, a matrimonial lawyer in whom he had great confidence. What really piqued my interest was Gordon's reference to Jay Goldberg, a lawyer who, by reputation, was tough and fierce, and who had successfully handled a major case for him. Goldberg had long been earning the plaudits of lawyers for his outstanding defense work. *New York* magazine once listed him among the ten "most powerful, talented, and fearsome" lawyers in the city, and a poll of attorneys and federal judges concluded that Goldberg was "a lawyer's lawyer who combined the various talents that made for an effective attorney." I called both Goldberg and Lotwin and arranged to meet with them that same day. I took an instant liking to this team and retained them on the spot, with Goldberg to act as lead counsel.

At our first official meeting, we discussed Ivana's likeliest course of action. It was clear that she would claim a half interest in my assets. This could have been disastrous for me. A person in the financial world who deals with banks and lending institutions needs to convey a certainty of ownership; any cloud on my title to property might have harmed me. Already the Industrial Bank of Japan, which had financed part of the Plaza, was becoming concerned that the hotel would go to Ivana in the divorce. The truth was, I was trying to steer a highly leveraged company through a bad economy, and any threat to my security would have scared my creditors.

Having learned about the importance of financial security from my professors at Wharton, I had entered into an agreement with Ivana before our marriage in 1977. I knew I would need to fix our rights to property in case the marriage ever floundered. We modified the agreement three times over the course of the next ten years to reflect Ivana's increasing contribution to the marriage and her growing role in the company. The last agreement was executed on December 24, 1987, after many meetings between our lawyers, Ivana, and me. The negotiations took over six months. It was stipulated that, in the event of our divorce, I was obligated to give her a lump sum of $10 million, $350,000 a year until her death, remarriage, or cohabitation, and our estate in Greenwich, Connecticut, which was worth some $12 million. In addition, Ivana would also receive a New York housing allowance of $4 million along with child support of $100,000 a year for each of our three children. All of this was exactly what Ivana had requested in a written list submitted to her own attorneys.

Goldberg and Lotwin were convinced that Ivana's strategy would be to claim that our agreement was in some way invalid. If she could prove this, her lawyer would be free to make increased demands. Their prediction proved correct. Ivana's first move was to declare that Lawrence Levner, the attorney who had represented her for all the prenuptial agreements, had not been representing her interests. I was advised that this tactic would be an enormous uphill battle for her, since Ivana had chosen Levner herself and established a social relationship with him over the years, sending him notes and gifts to show her appreciation for his efforts on her behalf. I had no relationship with him whatsoever, but I found him to be a vigorous lawyer who at all times served her interests well. I recalled that Ivana had also consulted with a Canadian lawyer before she signed the March 1977 contract, but I had no information regarding his name or location. Goldberg, knowing how lawyers operate, realized that this guy must have sent her a bill after realizing that he had conferred with the woman who later married Donald Trump. But Ivana was the only one in possession of this information. So, for the time being, this was a dead end.

I simply couldn't understand why Ivana was willing to engage in an expensive lawsuit challenging the validity of our contract since she had received perfectly sound legal advice. She had had counsel of her own choosing with whom she consulted every step of the way, and she had signed a document stating that she fully understood the terms. This was not a woman who had been forced at the last minute to sign something she didn't understand.

My lawyers assured me during meetings in February, March, and April of 1990 that my legal position was secure. Goldberg said that Ivana's attempt to break the agreement would be as effective as using a feather to knock down a skyscraper. In the meantime, there was a human side to this case that upset me very deeply. The press coverage throughout this entire time was so intense that I felt there was a serious risk to the emotional well-being of my children.

So many statements about my relationship with Ivana have hurt my family and me. The press was vicious and mean throughout the entire divorce; they never let up. I remember one horrible article in *Vanity Fair,* of course totally untrue, that claimed I was repulsed by Ivana after she supposedly had cosmetic surgery on a certain part of her body. "I wouldn't touch those things," I was quoted as having said. (Just for the record, all parts of her body were and are beautiful.) At first I was going to sue because it really seemed so unfair. Then I realized that if I did, I would just bring more attention to a lie that most people hadn't even read. I really didn't know what to do. I didn't even know whether to call Ivana. The statement must have been so hurtful to her. How was she to know that it was totally false? In the end, I chickened out and just didn't call; I figured she would never believe me anyway. But for the record, I never said it, never even thought it. It was a total lie. Ivana is a good woman, and for her to be hurt by a malicious story was sad.

Another example of such negligent reporting came with the infamous *Post* headline, where Marla was attributed as saying about me: THE BEST SEX I'VE EVER HAD. I guess I could've taken it as a great compliment, as many friends advised me to do, but I knew what it was—a cheap shot aimed at hurting everyone I cared about. It's amazing to me that journalists could sink so low as to completely disregard human feelings. How were Ivana and the kids supposed to react to such a low blow? Besides the feelings of those involved, the coverage was a disservice to the public. Important and historic events were unfolding in South Africa and Russia at the time. Nelson Mandela was being freed, and the tabloids were reporting on my personal misfortunes. Ridiculous. It was obvious that the *Post* was purveying sordid material in order to boost circulation, and it succeeded. They sold the hell out of that issue; you couldn't buy it anywhere. I suppose the public's fascination with us had to do with the times. Ivana and I represented a look, an age, a style, a certain success everyone

Ivana and I had some tough times, but she's a great woman. We shared some wonderful laughs together, and I couldn't ask for a better mother for my children.

seemed to be attracted to. I was supposedly the youngest billionaire at the time, and *Playgirl* had recently declared me to be one of the ten sexiest men of the decade. I was one of the few men to ever grace the cover of *Playboy*. It stands to reason that my personal life was newsworthy.

The press had me linked to dozens of other women. But as a friend so aptly stated, I couldn't have built my empire if I was having that kind of action. It was incredible, being intimately associated with women I had never heard of. Women themselves—some very famous—were linking themselves to me. I guess they wanted some of the publicity. They were calling. Their agents were calling. It was a circus! It was sick!

It got to the point where any woman I was seen with in public became the subject of rumors. To be honest, some of the rumors had some truth in them, but the stories usually went too far. Innocent women, such as Peggy Fleming, whom I barely know but have long admired for her gifts as a professional athlete, found themselves at the center of unfounded scandals. To make matters worse, some people took advantage of the hype just to get their names in the papers. Even Madonna, a master of hype in her own right, got in on the act.

When media speculation about my personal life was at its height, I attended a dinner honoring the legendary Diana Vreeland, which was held at the Plaza. Madonna arrived, dressed beautifully except for the combat boots, and mentioned to one of my managers that she wanted to say hello to me. I stopped by her table shortly afterward, and she introduced me to her boyfriend and her dancers, who, she said, were big fans of mine and wanted pictures and autographs. We all chatted for a short while, and I thought that was the end of it. When I read the *New York Post* the next day, I was furious to see a fabricated story that claimed I had asked Madonna out only to be turned down cold.

Madonna has an almost unequaled natural ability to promote herself. She knows how to be shocking and has created a brilliant façade that captures the imagination of millions. I was first introduced to her by my close friend Steve Rubell many years ago. Steve, who along with Ian Schrager had founded Studio 54, probably the hottest disco of all time, told me he thought Madonna would one day be a superstar, even though nobody at the time had heard of her. He was a great judge of people and turned out to be right.

I've come to like and respect Madonna. I spoke to her when she was doing the Versace photo shoot at Mar-a-Lago, which turned out to be a tremendous success, both artistically and commercially. I've got to hand it to her. There's nobody who works harder or longer than Madonna to keep it all going.

I don't know why, but I seem to bring out either the best or worst in women. During the divorce most of them, from a personal standpoint, were definitely at their worst. Even Katarina Witt, the great Olympic figure-skating champion, caused me some angst, despite the fact that I really didn't have any kind of relationship with her. After she had won her second gold medal and turned professional, she was quite in demand. Because I built and ran the Wollman Skating Rink in Central Park, which draws hundreds of thousands of skaters annually, I became something of a factor in the ice-skating business. One day I received a phone call from Katarina asking if she and Brian Boitano, another true champion, could come to my office to say hello. Being a sports fan, I said absolutely. Everything went well, and I was glad I'd taken time out to meet these two attractive young people. Some weeks later I received another call from Katarina, who was in Germany. She said she would soon be in New York and wondered if we could get together for lunch or dinner. I wasn't exactly sure why she wanted to see me, but I thought it was a nice gesture and agreed. We had a very pleasant lunch in my office, and that, I thought, was that.

However, Katarina got in touch with me a few times and invited me to see her opening-night performance at Madison Square Garden. I also attended the party celebrating the show with a friend. At one point Katarina asked me what I thought of the evening. I told her that, while I liked her skating, I thought the music she skated to was horrible. (In fact, the crowd much preferred Brian Boitano's performance to hers.) "I know you want to be artistic," I said, "but you really ought to choose music that's more mainstream, something people will enjoy." Katarina was not pleased with my comments, and I could see at a glance that steely German temperament. After that, every article written about Katarina Witt included claims that I had asked her out and she had turned me down. Finally, this lie turned up in a *People* story. The truth was that I had absolutely no interest in Katarina Witt, so I decided to take action. I wrote the following letter to *People,* and it was published in the next issue:

> Each and every time a story is written about Katarina Witt, my name is mentioned as a spurned suitor. The truth is that I hardly knew her except that on two occasions she came to my office, the first time with Brian Boitano, and the second time with her agent in order to have lunch and to discuss "endorsements." After that I was deluged with calls from Katarina asking me to go out with her (I have an abundance of witnesses), but I had no interest. She then invited me to a skating show at Madison Square Garden and to a party after the performance at which, because of my disinterest, she was very rude. Everyone is spurned at some time, but in this case it was Katarina, not Donald.

Not surprisingly, I never heard from Katarina again, nor was my name mentioned with hers in any future stories. I actually met her fairly recently doing an ice show at the Taj Mahal, and she was very nice—but I can't forget what she did.

Another strange incident began one night at a party given by a gentleman who owned a rather nice apartment in New York. Numerous attractive people were there, but I especially noticed one pretty lady in particular, whose name was Kim Alley. While the group was interesting, it wasn't *very* interesting, and somehow Kim and I spoke for about fifteen minutes.

One of the most intriguing things about this lady was her nickname. Everyone called her Alley Cat, and she was wearing a cap with ALLEY CAT written beautifully atop. I thought this was nice and a little bit wild—and certainly, with good names being somewhat scarce, interesting. As I was leaving the party I said good-bye to Alley Cat and another large group of people and headed with my group to the China Club on the West Side. While there, I noticed that Alley Cat had arrived with another group, but I paid no attention to her. The next day I was in my office working diligently when I received a call informing me that a woman was having a news conference announcing that she was my new girlfriend and that we were very much in love. I didn't know what was happening. It immediately became a huge story, garnering front-page headlines in the *Daily News* and the *New York Post* and television coverage like no one would believe. John Casablancas, the head of Elite Models, was actually prepared to sign Alley Cat based on the fact that he and I are friends and the incredible notoriety that the press had given her. What he didn't know was that the story wasn't true.

I was incensed because at the time Marla and I were getting along beautifully, and this would not encourage the continuance of a great relationship. What was I to do? I had this beautiful but crazy girl going around saying that she was my new girlfriend and that "Donald Trump is a great kisser." Everybody, including Marla, took this at face value. It was so preposterous that nobody believed it could be made up. Alley Cat was riding high. After two days of this I got a call from Geraldo Rivera, inviting me to be on a show entitled, as I remember, "The Life and Times of Donald Trump." I declined. Before hanging up, however, I asked him who would be on the show, and he named the people, including many gossip columnists and, last but not least, "my new girlfriend," the newly famous Alley Cat. This intrigued me, and although I was very busy that day I told him I would make a phone call to the show in order to confront her. When I did, I challenged her, essentially saying, "Come on, Alley Cat, you know this isn't true." She absolutely broke down on the show, almost immediately, and admitted the scam. I was amazed at my abilities of persuasion. I felt like Perry Mason must have felt during the last five minutes of his many trials. Alley Cat was discredited after that program, and I never heard from her again. Quite naturally, she was never hired by John Casablancas to be an Elite model. I don't know why I bring out this craziness in women, but somehow I do, and it's not always pretty.

As I said before, my primary concern was the pain these stories, generated by negligent reporting, caused my family. So despite what I believed to be the strength of my case, I told Goldberg to offer Kennedy $50 million to settle quickly with Ivana. My hope was to head off any full-fledged legal battle and insulate my children from further media attention. Unfortunately, there was no doubt in my mind that Kennedy wanted the lawsuit to go forward. If he'd won the suit, it would have been an opportunity to put his criminal work behind him and enter a new field in which he could get enormous amounts of publicity. But at whose expense? I had spoken to him on a number of occasions, often asking him to deliver conciliatory messages to my wife, only to talk to her later and have her act as if she hadn't gotten the message. I was becoming increasingly suspicious and wondered about his motives, and it came as no surprise when Jay told me that Kennedy had rejected the $50 million. He had demanded a lump sum of $150 million and threatened to have the 1987 marital agreement set aside and to tie up my financial interests for years. As soon as Kennedy refused the offer, Goldberg said to him, "You'll rue the day you turned your back on fifty million and ignored the interests of your client." Jay agreed with me that Kennedy had his own agenda. On May 3, 1990, Ivana brought a lawsuit against me. It would prove to be a costly mistake for her.

One of the main allegations of this lawsuit was that Ivana had been duped into signing the first prenuptial agreement in 1977. She claimed that she had been unfamiliar with the English language and argued that, if the first agreement was invalid, all subsequent agreements should also be declared invalid since they were the fruit of the first. The problem with this position was that I knew Ivana had a full understanding of the language back in 1977. Also she had had a lawyer at her side during all stages of the negotiations. As far as the agreements that followed our marriage were concerned, it seemed to me that they stood independently. Ivana's role in the business world during the years of our marriage had steadily increased. She had become proficient at analyzing financial statements and acted as the chief executive officer at Trump Castle Hotel and Casino in Atlantic City before becoming president of the Plaza Hotel. Everybody who met Ivana was impressed by her understanding of financial matters. Whether or not the March 1977 agreement was upheld, there was no doubt in my mind that all the agreements signed during our marriage, when Ivana was aided by her own counsel, would survive any court test.

Ivana's final claim—that she should be released from the terms of the 1987 agreement because my relationship with Marla had been so disruptive to our marriage—really concerned me at first, even though I didn't believe it was a strong legal argument. I was convinced that this had been made part of the case to afford Ivana and her attorneys an opportunity to explore the extent of my relationship with Marla and embarrass me. Ivana knew full well that I didn't leave her for Marla, but Kennedy convinced her to hire a hot-shot private eye from Texas to try to dig up anything he could about my relationship with Marla. They even explored the possibility that I had been seeing her before the 1987 agreement was signed. Ivana spent hundreds of thousands of dollars on this nonsense. I made no bones about my relationship with Marla, but I didn't want it all laid out in court depositions.

While Goldberg gave short shrift to Ivana's final claim and assured me that Judge Gangel-Jacob would have absolutely no trouble dismissing it, I was not so sure. I was familiar with Judge Gangel-Jacob's name, but only in a negative way. My brother in-law Jim Grau had appeared before her years ago in his own matrimonial suit. He complained bitterly that she had a decided bias in favor of the woman in any divorce proceeding. I was concerned that if the 1987 agreement could be jeopardized by what took place after we had executed it, then my property rights were indeed at risk.

The first blow to Ivana's case came when Judge Gangel-Jacob issued a decision that my postagreement conduct could not, in any way, affect the validity of the 1987 agreement. Kennedy's plan to use the matter of my relationship with Marla as a device for invalidating the agreement had failed. The case would now proceed on the less-than-convincing claim that the 1987 contract should be set aside because Ivana did not understand the terms and did not have independent or competent counsel from the time she first used Levner back in March of 1977.

Since Ivana had initiated the lawsuit, her deposition was taken first. During this proceeding she suffered a second blow. Goldberg asked her if she had ever consulted a Canadian lawyer prior to signing the 1977 agreement. She admitted that she had, but she no longer remembered his name or address and did not know how to contact him. But when Goldberg asked Ivana if she had received a bill from this lawyer following the consultation, something amazing happened. Ivana paused for a moment and then proceeded to pull a copy of the bill out of her purse. It not only listed his name and address but also indicated the large amount of time he had spent counseling her. With the discovery of this information, Goldberg assured me that our case was entirely secure. It was now completely clear that Ivana had extensive knowledge of our contract at the time we signed the original agreement. Further, all succeeding agreements were entered into when she was represented by counsel, and I had agreed to the monies she had asked for.

Judge Gangel-Jacob set a trial date for early April 1991. Goldberg prepared a trial book outlining the way in which he would cross-examine Ivana, detailing not only her consultations with lawyers prior to signing each of the agreements, but also her close relationship with Levner. Many witnesses were found to testify that Ivana was proficient in English as far back as 1977. All of her friends and associates knew she was a woman of independent mind; and because she had been in the business world for so many years, she had particular knowledge of financial matters. I firmly believed that there was no way we could lose this case and that Ivana would be bound to accept the monies provided for in the 1987 agreement.

Finally, she accepted the terms of our agreement—as I've said before, on possibly the worst financial day of my life—as I sat at my desk reading a *New York Times* cover story on my imminent demise.

The one good thing about going to court with Ivana would have been that I would not have had to pay the money for two or three years. I knew I would win the court case easily, so I would have the best of all worlds. By the time the payment came due, I felt, I would be in great financial shape again. I would easily be able to pay it. But now, here was Ivana, asking for $10 million in cash. This was incredible! On top of that, immediately after making the phone call to me, Ivana went to the press and told the reporters that she was now going to settle the case and was willing, almost as if she were doing me a favor, to take only $10 million plus the other things, which probably amounted to a total of $25 million. She worked hard to try and make it sound like she was doing me a great favor, trying to help me out.

The newspapers and televisions screamed, as far and away the biggest story of the day, that a settlement had been reached and that Ivana would, in fact, accept the agreement that she said she was defrauded into making. Under that headline almost all of the media predicted that it didn't matter, I would not be able to come up with the $10 million in cash anyway. But what I understand more than anything else is people. Deals are people, they are not deals, and if you don't have a deep understanding of people and their motives, you can never become a great dealmaker. I knew that when the going got really tough, and when bad financial stories would come out about me, coupled with the fact that I had proven to Ivana beyond any shadow of a doubt that she had no chance of winning her case, she would want to settle. I also knew that the settlement would come probably at the worst time, and lo and behold, I had reserved more than $10 million in cash for this event. While this was a tough time for everyone, and very few people had large amounts of cash, I knew the day would come when I would receive the call, "I vant my money." I also knew, however, that the ship could sink and I could be left with nothing. I wanted my children protected, and yes, I wanted Ivana protected—protected like she had never been protected before. This was very important to me.

Not long after my conversation with Ivana, Goldberg received a call from Kennedy confirming Ivana's desire to drop her suit. We agreed to divorce on mutually acceptable terms, but she would be limited financially to the terms of the 1987 agreement. On March 27, 1991, Goldberg, Lotwin, and I met with Ivana, Michael Kennedy, and attorneys from White & Case. I had the $10 million certified check in my pocket, but I would not agree to give it to Ivana until she and her attorneys confirmed, in writing, that the terms of the 1987 agreement were fair, reasonable, and valid. I found that the fight had been taken out of their entire team, although her attorneys still had enough energy to exact large legal fees from her. Despite the fact that

Ivana would be a very rich woman, I felt sorry for her. I reflected on the damage Ivana had caused herself during the two years of litigation. With attorneys' and private investigators' fees she had spent well over a million dollars. In the end she merely accepted what had been offered to her under the terms of a five-year-old agreement after passing up an opportunity to take $50 million. Ivana had also lost two years' worth of interest on the $10 million. From her perspective, the results were appalling.

Ivana was eager to get the check so she could catch a late flight to Palm Beach. She had planned a party for a number of her friends, including Barbara Walters. I left the lawyers to work out the details, went to New Jersey to attend a dinner honoring Muhammad Ali, and returned home close to midnight. That night she reaffirmed the 1987 agreement, including one provision that I cared a great deal about. Paragraph 10 stipulated that in exchange for the money I was to give her, Ivana was not to write any account of our life together or of my business affairs without first obtaining my written consent. This included the publication of diaries, memoirs, letters, interviews, and fictional accounts. If Ivana breached this clause in any way, I would no longer be obligated to uphold the financial end of the contract.

Following Ivana's receipt of her money, all that remained was for Judge Gangel-Jacob to embrace the settlement in what is known as the marital judgment. This turned the agreement into a court order. It was a mere formality, but I ran into a bit of bad luck, because Goldberg was out of the country when the lawyers submitted the papers to the judge in May 1991. In a move that surprised everyone, Judge Gangel-Jacob, without any prior notice to any of the lawyers, said that she felt the confidentiality clause improperly abridged Ivana's First Amendment rights to publish whatever she wanted. I called Goldberg, who was vacationing in Italy, and he assured me that he would successfully appeal the judge's action and that the clause would be restored to the marital judgment. I had a fierce competitor and a trusted friend in Jay Goldberg. In the earliest part of the divorce action, when the legal work and documentation were by far the most demanding, Jay refused to send me a bill. This is what loyalty and friendship are all about, and I will not forget him or his wonderful wife, Rema.

When Goldberg returned, he prepared the necessary papers to appeal the case to the appellate division, where five justices presided. By this time Ivana had decided to replace White & Case and Michael Kennedy. She hired Robert S. Cohen, a big-time matrimonial lawyer, to replace Kennedy. He prepared papers for the appellate division supporting the position taken by Judge Gangel-Jacob. The case was heard in February of 1992. Both Ivana and I attended the session because we wanted to see our lawyers in action and witness the court's decision firsthand. It was a media circus.

The court received my lawyer much more enthusiastically, and when I left the building that day I had no doubt that Judge Gangel-Jacob's opinion would be reversed. On June 12, 1992, a unanimous court ruled that the confidentiality clause must be reinstated in the marital judgment. Following this, Ivana lost faith in Cohen and dismissed him as well. The last I heard, he had brought a proceeding against Ivana trying to get her to pay his $50,000 fee. As an interesting footnote, Cohen has now been retained by Marla to represent her.

Despite this settlement, and two subsequent confirmations of the settlement when Ivana had various lawyers attempt to get the court to reverse its decision, Ivana went ahead and signed a very lucrative contract to publish two novels. The first, *For Love Alone,* showed up at number six on *The New York Times* best-seller list for three weeks and then disappeared despite a massive promotional blitz. The book was nothing more than a thinly veiled account of our marriage and breakup. I was furious that Ivana had broken our contract after we'd been through so much to establish the terms of the confidentiality clause. After the book came out, I did an interview with Howard Stern, who noted, "You know, it's really disgusting what happened with your wife. You paid her twenty-five million dollars to get her to shut up, and she didn't. If you had a judge who was fair, or who had some guts—if the laws meant anything—you'd get your twenty-five million back." A lot of people told me just that, and I agreed with them. With that much money in her bank account, there were a lot of things Ivana could have been doing instead of writing gossip "fiction."

Ivana really didn't treat me fairly, and she knows this. In the worst financial period of my life I gave her a big check, a beautiful house, and total financial security. I didn't have to do it. I could've delayed to a point where no money would've been paid, or at least, a lot less. I didn't want to do this. I wanted to make sure that she and my children had total financial security. Despite this, before the settlement and documents were even dry, Ivana built a small cottage industry on my back. She would appear on talk shows and make speeches about how other women should follow her lead. She would talk about how she survived, when in actuality, all I did was pay what I agreed to pay and live up to every inch of the agreement. All I did was act honorably and make sure that my family was protected. I would laugh as I watched Ivana on Larry King and other shows, telling other women the how-to's of getting divorced and living life afterward. On these shows I would see women left with four or five children whose husbands had moved to another state. Some husbands would just disappear, leaving their wives stranded with no money. And there sat Ivana in her fancy dresses, all paid for by me, telling these women how to live.

What also upsets me about Ivana is her little business. While it does okay, it always fascinated me that she would talk about herself as a businesswoman and not as someone who received a large settlement from her husband. Trust me, she would not exchange the business for the settlement. In fact, when she got married to Riccardo Mazzuchelli, for some reason she allowed him to pierce the corporate veil and obtain a piece of her company. Why she did this, I don't know, but if we were dealing with something large and powerful, that certainly would not have happened.

Ivana never gave me credit for how good I was to her. She tried to minimize to almost nothing everything that I did for her. She claimed she made all of her money through business, which is total nonsense. Ivana always calls me when she needs help—like with her boat and with her breakup with Mazzuchelli—and then, after I get her straightened out, she forgets to say thank you.

Ivana said she would never use the name Trump—she didn't need it—she would go solely by Ivana. However, she is always referred to as Ivana Trump, and was even during her marriage to Mazzuchelli. She tried to play down the name Trump, but when going by Ivana alone didn't work, she immediately switched back. Worse, after telling everybody she wouldn't use my name, she came out with a book with the name Ivana Trump in big letters, right on the front cover. She realized very soon that the Trump name is a great big asset.

Despite all of this, I still think of Ivana as a very kind and good woman. I also think she has the instincts and drive of a good manager. She is focused and she is a perfectionist. Without a doubt, Ivana is a great mother and an okay businesswoman. When people break up it is rarely one person's fault; more likely it's a joint "effort." In the case of our breakup, while it is perceived to have been my idea, there are always many reasons. If you don't look forward to going home at night, perhaps the marriage just doesn't work. My big mistake with Ivana was taking her out of the role of wife and allowing her to run one of my casinos in Atlantic City, then the Plaza Hotel. While she did an excellent job at both, I could have hired a manager who also would've done a very good job. The problem was, work was all she wanted to talk about. When I got home at night, rather than talking about the softer subjects of life, she wanted to tell me how well the

Plaza was doing, or what a great day the casino had. I really appreciated all of her efforts, but it was just too much. I work from six o'clock in the morning until seven or eight o'clock at night; to come home and hear more was just not tolerable. And Ivana just wouldn't stop. She had so much energy, and it wasn't simply, "We had a good day today"; she had to relate everything that happened during the day, in detail, and then everything that was planned for the following days and weeks. I will never again give a wife responsibility within my business. Ivana worked very hard, and I appreciated the effort, but I soon began to realize that I was married to a businessperson rather than a wife. It wasn't her fault, but I really believe it wasn't my fault either. It was just something that happened.

After the divorce settlement, I began to restructure my empire. But during this crucial time, another important event was unfolding. My relationship with Marla began to develop and grow. There were several misunderstandings on the way, leading to a series of breakups and subsequent rekindlings. The main issue of contention between us was that Marla wanted to be married as quickly as possible. I, on the other hand, still had my doubts—and my doubts proved to be well founded.

At the time my marriage with Ivana ended, most people were misled by the press into thinking that it was Marla who caused the breakup. What really served as a catalyst to the separation, however, was the death of three of my top executives in a helicopter accident in October of 1989. The morning of the tragedy, they met with me in my Trump Tower office, then left to fly down to Atlantic City. It was unbelievable: They were sitting right in front of my desk in the morning, and then an hour later the chopper went down. I would have been with them if it wasn't for the fact that that afternoon I had a meeting I could not easily break with a guy I truly hated (now when I see this man I always profess my love—who says there's no such thing as luck?). The whole experience showed me how short and how fragile life is. It also made me take stock of my personal life. Ivana and I had been growing apart for a long time; it just took something this drastic for one of us to truly notice it. I suppose that's what prompted me to accept that the marriage was over when I received the news of the press leak on the way home from Tokyo.

Strangely enough, it was another tragedy that led to my decision to marry Marla. Despite my love for her, the problems I had had with my previous marriage made me a little gunshy. Marla is beautiful and talented. Her role on Broadway in *The Will Rogers Follies* was enough to make not only me, but the public, realize that she was a good actress. The reason she stopped performing in this role was a nice one—the birth of our daughter, Tiffany. However, despite her wonderful qualities and our beautiful child, marriage still seemed far off. One day something happened to change all of this. The Long Island Rail Road was assaulted by a crazed gunman who fired indiscriminately on a car full of passengers. Once again I was reminded of the fragility of life. Everything can end so quickly, so abruptly. Marla had always been there for me, she had always loved me. Shortly after this horrible incident, Marla and I got married.

Since my previous divorce settlement had caused such strife, I asked Marla to sign a prenuptial agreement negotiated by Stanford Lotwin, the attorney who had been so helpful during the proceedings. It was obvious that Marla was opposed to the agreement, but she also understood why it was important to me. She had a lawyer review its contents in great detail and agreed to the provisions set forth in the agreement. Our wedding date was set: December 20, 1993.

The wedding was beautiful. The ceremony was held at the Plaza and performed by the Reverend Arthur Caliandro. He tried his best to keep it traditional and religious despite the hundreds of press photographers waiting outside. More than a thousand friends and family members attended. Traffic around the hotel was backed up for blocks;

no one could get through. White orchids abounded in the Grand Ball-room, where the wedding took place. Chamber music played as every-one waited for Marla to walk down the aisle. And when she did, she was radiant. She was wearing a white Carolina Herrera dress and a $2 million diamond tiara designed by Harry Winston. After the wed-ding, everyone moved into the reception room. They were amazed by the cake—it was six feet tall, made of nineteen individual cakes, each one filled with vanilla cream. Every detail was attended to; the wed-ding was one of the biggest of our time. The caviar alone cost me over $60,000. I'm happy to say that the wedding and reception were a com-plete success; the food and champagne were magnificent. Because we knew that there was no way our guests could finish this feast, Marla and I decided to reach out to the less fortunate. The leftovers—more than five hundred pounds—were donated to the McAuley Mission, where those in need dined on steaks, salmon, lamb, shrimp, beef ribs, and caviar.

My marriage to Marla lasted three and a half years. Sadly, like so many couples these days, we drifted apart. Our lifestyles became less and less compatible. We wanted different things. Marla was content when it was just her, Tiffany, and me. I, on the other hand, realized that business needed to be taken care of constantly. When two people have such a difference in opinion regarding the lifestyle they want to lead, there is no longer any reason to stay together.

I hope Marla and I will never go through the strife that Ivana and I endured, but who knows? I learned my lesson well. The provisions in case of our separation were clearly spelled out. Tiffany will be more than amply provided for. It can never be said that my children are not my first priority.

Ivana and Marla both taught me a great deal about myself and my interests. The personal relationships I've had with both can never be fully understood by anyone, despite the fact that they have been

Donato's Studio

My mother was always at my side, even at New York Military Academy.

dragged through the press. One thing I have learned: There is high maintenance. There is low maintenance. I want no maintenance.

As for now, I have decided to take a break from romance. Don't get me wrong, everyone seems to think they know the perfect woman for me—I've gotten more suggestions than I can keep track of. I'll never say that I'm not interested in beginning a new relationship, it's just not one of my first priorities at the moment.

I love women. They've come in to my life. They've gone out of my life. Even those who have exited somewhat ungracefully still have a place in my heart. I only have one regret in the women department—that I never had the opportunity to court Lady Diana Spencer. I met her on a number of occasions. I couldn't help but notice how she moved people. She lit up the room with her charm, her presence. She was a genuine princess—a dream lady. She'll truly be missed.

1997 Copyright, NYP Holdings, Inc. Reprinted with permission from the New York Post.

THE ART OF THE PRENUP:

THE ENGAGEMENT WRING

A PRENUPTIAL AGREEMENT IS A TERRIBLE, VICIOUS, AND
ugly document that spells out the terms and conditions of a divorce
long before the event itself. Probably the worst thing about a prenuptial agreement is that it becomes, in many cases, a self-fulfilling
prophecy. People who have prenups seem predisposed to divorce; and
surveys have indicated that this is true. A couple who signs a prenuptial agreement is approximately 50 percent more likely to divorce

than couples who don't. In order to make the statistic look a little friendlier, however, it must be pointed out that without a prenuptial agreement it can be so complicated and financially wrenching to split that many decide it is better to remain being unhappily married than go through the trauma of divorce.

For example, due to the vastness and complexity of my business, it would have taken ten or fifteen years in many different courts, states, and perhaps even countries to finalize my situation with either Ivana or Marla. My financial life would have been officially over, and certainly I wouldn't be able to write a book. Many millions would have been paid to lawyers. It would have been ridiculous. In terms of wheeling and dealing, which is essentially my life, I would've been reduced to court orders and litigation. My business would have been in total disarray.

During my first divorce, Ivana tried to put liens on almost all of my properties, at the most critical financial time of my life. If she had succeeded in this, I would not have been able to deal myself out of a very tough financial situation. Rather, I would have had to go to her for approval to sell anything. For instance, when I needed to sell my yacht in order to raise cash or when I sold the Trump Shuttle in order to get out of those liabilities, I would have needed her permission. When I made my great deal on the Plaza Hotel, I would have had to go to Ivana, not an easy thing in and of itself, and ask for her approval. This would have been a ludicrous situation for me or anyone else. Certainly, at that time of her life, Ivana would not have wanted to see me do well. Therefore, she would have had no real inclination to approve the deal unless I gave her an extraordinary edge. Since I had the prenup, the court wiped out the liens as soon as they were filed.

In deciding to write about prenuptial agreements, I was faced with the dilemma of where the subject fit in the book. Do I put it under Women in my Life, Ingredients for Success, or just give it its own chapter? I decided to do the separate chapter because it covers all of the territory. It certainly covers marriage and women, but it also has a lot to do with the ingredients for success—and perhaps, even more so, the ingredients to making a financial comeback.

My comeback would have been totally impossible had I not had fully executed and well-drawn prenuptial agreements with both Ivana and Marla. The great thing about a prenuptial agreement is that you go into it with all sides properly protected by competent counsel. Everybody signs it, happy or not. Then an extraordinary thing happens: You split up, and the women try to act like they didn't know what they were doing when they signed the document. Witness Ivana, a very sophisticated person, fighting long and hard in her claim that she didn't speak English well enough to understand what she was signing. Marla's case will be interesting and will tell me a lot about her.

This book is being written at a very delicate time in my relationship with Marla. Many lawyers are circling her in order to gain fame and fortune; they're trying to convince her to protest our agreement. I have already been contacted by Robert Cohen, one of Ivana's former lawyers. He is a decent guy. Let's see where he takes Marla. Money is being placed on both sides of the betting table as to whether or not she'll fight our prenup. By the time this book is out you will probably have the answer. In order to protect myself against a legal battle, particularly against what Ivana did when I was forced to spend a great amount in legal fees in order to win, I took certain precautions. I added a clause to my contract with Marla that states, in effect, that if she protests this prenuptial agreement and loses, she has to pay my legal fees. They will be very substantial, perhaps even more than the amount I'd be paying her. For all those people who have read this book, I hope you enjoy watching. I won't. And remember, it is only the lawyers who come out on top.

The most difficult aspect of the prenuptial agreement is informing your future wife (or husband): I love you very much, but just in case things don't work out, this is what you will get in the divorce.

There are basically three types of women and reactions. One is the good woman who very much loves her future husband, solely for himself, but refuses to sign the agreement on principle. I fully understand this, but the man should take a pass anyway and find someone else. The other is the calculating woman who refuses to sign the prenuptial agreement because she is expecting to take advantage of the poor, unsuspecting sucker she's got in her grasp. There is also the woman who will openly and quickly sign a prenuptial agreement in order to make a quick hit and take the money given to her. I have seen this on two occasions. I was surprised, especially having known one of the women, that these people so openly and quickly negotiated out a deal and then just as quickly dissolved the marriage. They had a nice clean split and got a fat check for very little work. This must sound awfully sinister to those of you who lead a more normal life than I do, but in my world this kind of crap happens all the time. People are really vicious, and no place are they more vicious than in their relationships with the opposite sex.

The fact is that time moves on and people change. You can be deeply in love when you get married, but a number of years later you just don't care to spend your life with that person anymore. When you have a prenuptial agreement, you're able to get out of the situation. It is not the end-all, and even with a prenup, a separation or a divorce is not easy. But without the prenup, the divorce becomes almost impossible with the way the laws are written today.

There is no question that approaching your future spouse about a prenup is very difficult. I have heard of cases where women break down into total hysteria. I have even heard of a case where a man was ordered to sign one in order to protect the wealth of the woman and he started crying. Actually, I know the guy in question, and I know how hard he worked to land this particular very wealthy lady. I have no doubt in my mind that he was only crying because her representatives were able to nip his act in the bud. Due to the fact that he was to get nothing in case of divorce, he decided to break things off—after working two and a half years to hit paydirt.

You have to protect yourself. You never know how the dynamics in a marriage will play out. Marla was always wanting me to spend more time with her. "Why can't you be home at five o'clock like other husbands?" she would ask. Sometimes, when I was in the wrong mood, I would give a very materialistic answer. "Look, I like working. You don't mind traveling around in beautiful helicopters and airplanes, and you don't mind living at the top of Trump Tower, or at Mar-a-Lago, or traveling to the best hotels, or shopping in the best stores and never having to worry about money, do you? If you want me to be home at five o'clock, maybe these other things wouldn't happen and you'd be complaining about that, too. Why would you want to take something that I enjoy and change it?" I always viewed her whys as being very selfish, but the fact is, in a marriage both sides have to be happy. If they're not, it's just not going to work.

Often, I will tell friends whose wives are constantly nagging them about this or that that they're better off leaving and cutting their losses. I'm not a great believer in always trying to work things out, because it just doesn't happen that way. For a man to be successful he needs support at home, just like my father had from my mother, not someone who is always griping and bitching. When a man has to endure a woman who is not supportive and complains constantly about his not being home enough or not being attentive enough, he will not be very successful unless he is able to cut the cord.

I recently played golf with one of the most brilliant men on Wall Street, the head of Morgan Stanley, John Mack. John is a good friend of mine who is married to a fabulous woman. Christy is totally supportive of the long, hard hours he works. John was telling me that after our game he was going to see one of his men. This particular man had the potential to be a star at Morgan Stanley, but he was having tremendous difficulty with his wife. She always complained that he was working too hard and too long and wasn't devoting enough time or energy to her. Without any further discussion, I looked at John and said, "Tell the man to lose the wife. There is no hope for that marriage. Tell him if he stays, he'll do a lousy job for you."

John looked at me and, being the good family man that he is, disagreed. He thought everything would work out fine and was looking forward to seeing them both, in order to get things on track. I told John that I didn't want to sound cold or cynical, but I knew the marriage just wasn't going to work. If the woman was inclined this way, she was not going to change. I actually told John to pull the young man aside and tell him that it was me who made this recommendation: If he doesn't lose the ballbreaker, his career will go nowhere. I have no doubt that I will be proven right in the long run, but I truly respect John for giving it the old college try.

Another example is a friend of mine who is a great golfer. He plays on the pro golf tour and has been getting better and better each time he goes out—until recently—although he is not yet a household name. As a pretty good athlete and golfer myself, I can tell you his potential is tremendous, but he does have one very big problem—his wife. She complains incessantly, despite living in a beautiful house in a beautiful community, that he is not home enough to satisfy her needs. She'll call him in the middle of a tournament and start crying that she wants him back, now. He explains to her that he is a touring professional, with the word *touring* strongly emphasized. As such he has to travel the country and even the world in order to play golf and bring home money. He explains that they'll have lots of time to be together during the off season and in the years ahead, but right now he's touring. This never satisfies her.

All this strife has put a lot of pressure on him, and in fact, his game has gone downhill lately. He called me to ask what he should do, and I told him very simply that he had a choice. He could go home and be with his wife and perhaps make her happy. However, he would always harbor a huge disgust toward her for not giving him his chance at greatness. In this case, the marriage probably wouldn't work anyway. The other alternative would be to cut her loose: "Tell her to find a guy who's going to be better for her then you." She won't find it easy and the grass will not be greener, I told him, but in my opinion, she is very selfish and he would do much better without her. Find a woman who is supportive, because there is nothing better than a supportive woman.

"You've got a chance to do great," I told him, "but you'll never be great married to this woman. She'll drive you totally crazy and directly cause your failure at something in which you have a tremendous God-given ability. If she wants a husband who's home all the time, let her find somebody else."

So far he hasn't taken my advice, but I predict that he soon will. The other night I got a call from him saying that she's gotten worse than ever.

I could go on forever about the virtues and liabilities of a prenuptial agreement, but in a nutshell, anyone of wealth, especially substantial wealth, and even more important, wealth that's in a complicated business form, should be institutionalized if he or she gets married without one. This book is called *The Art of the Comeback*, and I know firsthand that you can't come back if you're spending 100 percent of your time fighting with a spouse for your sanity and financial life.

The massive West Side Railroad Yards. After fifteen years of false starts, it is now well under way.

THE REALLY BIG ONE:

BREAKING GROUND

NOTHING IS MORE UNFAIR OR RIDICULOUS THAN THE MIND-less bureaucracy of New York local government. Red tape. Meetings. Proposals. Amended proposals. Environmental-impact studies. Votes. Amended environmental-impact studies. More votes. Follow-up meetings ad nauseam. Seriously, the approval process leaves me—and everyone else for that matter—numb. I just want to build. After all, that's what I do best.

Ten years. It took me ten frustrating years to break ground on the West Side Railroad Yards project, comprising Television City, Trump City, Trump Boulevard, and Riverside South. A wild, almost unbelievable tale spins out over two decades, a tale of pointless bureaucracy, failed promises, friendship, betrayal, loyalty, and duplicity—all ending in victory. We broke ground early this year. This tale of triumph often features strange and colorful characters. And the tale has a moral, gleaned by Herbert Muschamp, the wonderful and well-respected architecture critic for *The New York Times,* in an article about the project in 1996: "What does it say about the state of urban policy that it takes such an enormous project—virtually a small city—to fix one subway station? What does it say when it takes a luxury housing developer to create affordable housing?" Welcome to the drama of Riverside South.

Who knew in 1974, when I first bought the West Side Railroad Yards (I sold it and then bought it back years later)—a seventy-six-acre stretch of undeveloped land right next to the Hudson River—that I'd still be fighting to build today. It's absurd. Manhattanites are suffocating—there's a desperate demand for housing. Yesterday I picked up *The New York Times.* Cover story: HOUSING SHORTAGE WILL WORSEN IN 1998. I read on. Ninety-eight percent of apartments in New York City are occupied. Rents have never been higher. Even if you can find an apartment, the writer notes, chances are you can't afford it. I look up from the paper. I walk to the window of my penthouse atop Trump Tower. Just across the park, flanking the east side of the Hudson River, sits my enormous piece of land, poised for development. For seventy-five years, developers—some great, some not—have tried to build on this land, and now the process has begun.

My mind drifts back to 1982. I'd just repurchased the land from Francesco Macri, a great Argentine businessman. He'd had a hard time with the zoning process. You can't really do business in New York if you don't understand New York—its politics, the people, the pulse.

Some of the other developers were so desperate to get approvals that they gave away more than $200 million in concessions. No one, and I mean no one, could make enough money to turn a profit on a deal like that. So when the last round hit the wall—the banks shut them down—I decided to step in with a clean slate. I didn't want to be held accountable for past mistakes, so I threw away the approvals they'd sold their souls to acquire. It was time to design.

I developed a plan called Television City, a bold, aggressive blueprint that included the world's tallest building and acres of studio space. At the time, NBC was threatening to move out of Manhattan to somewhere in New Jersey. In typical form, the city government didn't seem all that concerned about losing more than four thousand jobs. Ed Koch & Company didn't flinch at saying good-bye to half a billion a year in revenues and great prestige. I realize now that it was personal. Ed Koch didn't like me. He may have respected me, but he sure didn't like me.

Our relationship went south for one reason: the Wollman Rink in Central Park. You may remember the tale. Local government had been trying for seven years—and $20 million—to get that thing rebuilt. In 1986, I stepped in, and—with $2 million, or 10 percent of the city's dollars—New Yorkers were gliding across the ice four months later. Koch was humiliated. He took it personally. Rather than compliment me on saving the Wollman Rink, one of the great bureaucratic disasters in New York City history, Ed Koch tried to make light of my triumph by saying that the city could have done the same thing, that is, build the rink in four months rather than in seven years, if only it were not forced to go through bureaucratic red tape. This was nonsense, and everyone knew it, but nevertheless, Ed's feeling toward me came out loud and clear. He felt I'd shown him up, and from that point forward my relationship with Ed Koch was the pits.

I couldn't understand why Koch didn't see NBC's potential move as a crisis. He seemed almost blasé about it. I presented my plan to

Koch and asked him, as mayor, for his support—to help me convince NBC to move to my site. He did the opposite. Koch slammed me every chance he got. And people began to get wind of it. That summer *The Wall Street Journal* ran an editorial that claimed Koch's irrational behavior was based on ego and, oddly enough, jealousy. Television City was clearly good for New York, and everyone knew it—not just the editorial writers at the *Journal.* Koch's pettiness cost the city, a city he'd sworn to serve, in jobs, tax revenues, and housing.

I believe in doing things big. I tell my kids: If you're going to do it, go for it. Make it the biggest, make it the best. This philosophy didn't sit well with the residents of the Upper West Side. They were crawling all over me with mostly perfunctory opposition. They just didn't like the idea of having me in their backyard. Also, keep in mind that a lot of the people who sit on these boards and organize these coalitions basically just don't have enough to do. I guess opposing my plan gave them a sense of purpose. They saw power. They wanted some too.

The Wollman Rink was zero stories tall but one of my great successes.

Mayor Giuliani and parks commissioner Henry Stern presented me with this plaque in recognition of my work on Wollman Rink, which would still be a construction site if I had not saved it.

Creating a city within a city takes vision. I have a vision. And I wanted to use it, not be embroiled in endless controversy and bureaucracy. I'll never forget the day my colleague Norma handed me a letter from Steven Rockefeller. He must have heard about my travails, because it was a note of encouragement. He had enclosed an architecture review of Rockefeller Center while it was still on the drawing board back in 1931. Critics called it a "weakly conceived romantic chaos" that represented the "sorriest failure of imagination and intelligence in modern American architecture." The letter read simply, "Keep the faith and stay on track, Donald. All the best, Steve."

The small group of devout enemies toward my project was led by Madeleine Palaise, a community activist of virtually no vision who unfortunately had nothing but time on her hands. She had fought the

An artist's rendering of the former railroad yards at its completion.

project long before I had arrived and had made life difficult for previous developers. I always thought I could have made a deal with her, but a lot would have had to be sacrificed in the job, and the development never would have been as good as it is today. So I took her on. And despite her lawsuits and howling at every front, she was easy to defeat.

Often you appreciate a good fight and you respect your opponent. But in this case I really liked grinding her into the ground. The Madeleine Palaises of the world are, in my opinion, very bad for New York. They fight people at every turn, hoping for attention—almost nothing else. The best way to deal with them is to beat them—and that's what I did.

It just didn't make sense. Not many people know this, but before the Depression, the rich preferred to live in the newest buildings. New construction created the most desirable housing. For some reason this attitude has changed. Perhaps it's people's obsession with nostalgia. Who knows? Who cares? For me it's a tremendous hassle. Because when the city requires builders to follow the guidelines of outmoded styles, using outmoded materials, it stifles architectural expression.

So I rolled up my shirtsleeves and prepared for war. I identified my bloodiest battle: the Uniform Land Use Review Process (or ULURP). ULURP is an impossible situation. All applicants are approved by the Board of Estimate, composed of the five borough presidents, the city council president, and the comptroller. In order to move from one level to the next in the approval process—from the community board to the borough president to the City Planning Commission and so on—the applicant is forced to negotiate blind, clueless as to the opponent's demands. It's a circus. And it often produces approval packages that are essentially unbuildable.

Koch decided he'd change all this. I was optimistic—until I learned of his plan. In his infinite wisdom, Koch created yet another bureaucratic entity, the Charter Revision Commission, and placed Frederick A. O. Schwarz, heir to the FAO Schwarz fortune, at the helm.

To put it bluntly, it was a complete disaster. The process became more cumbersome, expensive, and time-consuming than ever. I was appalled. Nothing, I had thought, could have made this process more inefficient, more ill-conceived, but I was wrong. A cover article in *The New York Times* cooed that F.A.O. Schwarz had turned his attention away from development to "the birds, the bees, the trees, and toxic dumps." How pathetic. I forged on, hitting wall after wall.

Then, just as I was about to bail out, a couple of prominent architects presented a plan to the city called "the Civic Alternative." It had the support of the civic groups and the West Side residents. My curiosity was piqued. I decided to snoop around.

It was right around Christmas, so I had umpteen Christmas parties to attend. I don't much like parties. I like to work. Luckily, during at least one, I was able to do both. I ran into a friend, Stephen Swid, at Cravath, Swaine & Moore's annual Christmas cocktail bash. Steve headed up the Municipal Arts Society. I assumed he might have the inside track on the details of the alternative plan. We agreed to meet a few days before Christmas to discuss it.

The meeting was tense. I found myself face-to-face with Bruce Simon of WestPride, the West Side residents coalition, Linda David-off of the Parks Council, Kent Barwick of the Municipal Arts Society, and other opponents to Riverside South. They presented the plan. I was impressed, particularly with one aspect—the idea of relocating the existing Miller Highway in an arc toward the east away from the Hudson River. Moving the highway would open up Manhattan to the water. It would create more space for a park. We'd finally have public access to the waterfront. It was a great idea but not that viable. The city was ready to spend $63 million fixing up the highway, but moving it would cost an extra $100 million at least.

I seriously considered embracing the Civic Alternative and giving up Riverside South. My execs urged me not to quit. Riverside South was only one or two weeks away from certification. Essentially, I was on my opponent's eight-yard line. It was a tough call. After five years and millions of dollars I was being offered a new team with a better game plan, except I'd be moving the ball back to the twenty-yard line. With absolutely no guarantees. It wasn't even a decision between field goal and touchdown. I could end up with nothing.

I thought about it for days. I went back to the drawing board. Then I made my decision. If the civics gave me guarantees, I'd join them. I asked the city for more support. I wanted certainty that the administration and the elected officials would back me up. I got my Memorandum of Understanding, and the civics got me. I didn't surprise anyone as much as I surprised myself.

We put together a feisty team: Linda Davidoff, Bruce Simon, Kent Barwick, Richard Anderson of the Regional Plan Association, Frances Beinecke of the Natural Resources Defense Council, Peter Wright of the Riverside Park Fund, Richard Kahan of the Urban

Development Corporation, and me. Richard Kahan was in charge. That gave me great comfort. I trusted him and respected his ability. He thinks like a businessman but also had a great vision for the site. Those were long, grueling months. After I decided to go with the civics, I went around Manhattan telling people this was either the dumbest or the smartest decision I'd ever made in business. I was getting into bed with my enemies, but I had found, during our negotiations, that these "enemies" were in actuality very good people.

Many of them had devoted years of their life to specific areas, for example, Linda Davidoff to the parks, and all of them gave me great ideas. Also, these members were highly respected by the politicians. I found that with them, things could get done that a developer would never ask for. The truth is, and I am now very glad to admit it, the project would never have been as good without the input given by the civics.

So on March 5, 1991, my development was really born. Mayor Dinkins and civic leaders throughout the city held a major news conference at which it was announced that an agreement had been struck with me: For agreeing to move the West Side Highway inland, a feat to be paid for by government, the city and the seven leading civic associations within the state of New York would support my project and speed it through the bureaucracy of the New York City zoning process. The West Side of Manhattan, at the insistence of the various civic leaders and groups, was to get a great and unencumbered thirty-acre park fronting the Hudson River. And I was to get speed and certainty of approval.

It sounded like a good deal to me, but interestingly, in the end, the civics were badly hurt by a small group of political leaders headed by Jerry Nadler, the local congressman, who fought against the funding for the highway after the money had been virtually obtained. The end result was that I got my zoning, in rapid fashion, and the civics and West Side residents did not get their park, for which they'd fought so hard and so long. While this was good for me, it was extremely unfair to them.

Sometimes I can't believe it. My deal. Negotiated. Done. And *with* the civics, no less. I hadn't made my usual slew of enemies. We'd made a few compromises but nothing major: nine million square feet of space, 5,600 apartments. We assured West Side residents with design guidelines to ensure compatibility between Riverside South and the surrounding neighborhoods. I agreed to manage the public park if it was approved. It was the largest single development ever undertaken by the private sector in New York City—the largest job ever approved by the New York City Planning Commission. We'd won.

And we got great feedback. Paul Goldberger of *The New York Times* wrote, "Riverside South is right. . . . It is intelligently tied in to the existing city, yet it holds the promise of being a special, even a unique place." Governor Cuomo, who had backed us all along, renewed his commitment. Mayor Dinkins was behind us. Almost everybody was behind us, in fact, other than a small band of people, such as Jerry Nadler and some of the local politicians.

One of the more interesting stories I tell—one that sheds a lot of light on New York City politics—is that during the early years of the development, I gave political support to Jerry Nadler. No deals were made, but nevertheless, I was his supporter. Amazingly, during this time he never once opposed the job, even when I was proposing the world's tallest building. When things got tight for me in the early 1990s and I stopped supporting him, only because I didn't have the time, patience, and didn't want to waste the money, he became my opponent. And not just an opponent in general, he became an opponent of Riverside South, the Civic Alternative—a much more popular plan than anything previously proposed on the site. Interesting how politics work, isn't it? If I support him, he likes one-hundred story buildings. If I don't, he fights me on something that everybody wants.

In truth, Nadler was neither for nor against the highway—he just wanted to derail my project. What he didn't realize was that he was making it much less expensive for me to build. Now that the job has started, the Upper West Side is extremely angry with Congressman Nadler. Because I got my job and they didn't get their park.

On May 18, 1992, fourteen months after our announcement, we were ready to begin the seven months of formal, public review. The last stand. And it was a battle. Upper West Side residents are notoriously—and loudly—active politically. They felt betrayed that the civics had joined me. Then City Council president Andrew Stein pulled the rug out from under me. (I'll get to that later.) Everyone seemed to be overlooking the obvious, most crucial point: economics. At the time, unemployment in New York had hit 11.5 percent. Construction was at a virtual standstill. Riverside South had the potential to create fifty thousand construction jobs and well over five thousand permanent jobs—not to mention the added tax dollars.

Dinkins and Cuomo got that. The editorial writers at the *New York Post* got it. The editorial read, "Today, blocking development for reasons devoid of logic seems downright suicidal. Donald Trump has gone well beyond halfway in an effort to satisfy his foes."

So I'd gotten the support of *some* of the media. I went after labor. I set up a meeting of New York's major union leaders, to build support. Ten thousand construction workers marched on City Hall, demanding the approval of Trump City. Eddie Malloy and the heads of the various construction unions were terrific in their push for more jobs.

Despite the support, the Community Board voted 35–1 against the plan. No surprise. I realized I had to take on—and eventually woo—Ruth Messinger. I have a great deal of respect for Ruth. As

Manhattan borough president, her life has got to be hell. Every day she deals with guiding people through the considerations of public policy, vicious political ambitions, the settling of old scores, and endless politicking. It's worthy of a Jackie Collins novel: A mayoral hopeful has cast aside his longtime friend in search of votes. Borough presidents ceaselessly vow to protect their home turf. A well-known socialite and another official trade passionate charges of selling out and caving in. Queens is worried about the proposed television studio competing with Silvercup Studios in Astoria. The Bronx wants $7 million it was promised under a previous plan for the site. And Brooklyn seems to want to pay Ruth back for an earlier vote against a development.

My strategy with Ruth: Kill her with kindness—in the form of affordable housing. I welcomed the chance to open up Riverside South to more people. Messinger suggested making 20 percent of the housing units "affordable." With no government assistance, a minimum of 12 percent of affordable housing would be required—6 percent low-income, 3 percent moderate-income, and 3 percent middle-income. Some of the demands were unreasonable. For instance, the city asked me to foot the whole bill for the repairs on the Seventy-second Street subway station: $35 million. I said forget it.

Once we had Ruth Messinger's vote we were ready for the ULURP endgame. We turned up the heat. I had to please the commission and the council without committing to an unbuildable project. In the end I agreed to reduce the size of the development from 8.3 million to 7.9 million square feet. I also pledged to give the Metropolitan Transit Authority $5 million.

That was it. The Planning Commission approved us, 12–0. Frankly, I was surprised by the unanimous vote. First, it's exceedingly rare, even on the rosiest of projects. Second, I had a few loud opponents, then borough president Andrew Stein and a well-known socialite, Amanda Burden. Stein and I had been friends for fifteen years. I'd contributed hundreds of thousands of dollars to his campaigns. I never once asked for favors. He offered. "I'll always support you," he'd say. "Don't you worry about a thing, Donny." It's ironic. I never, not once, asked Andy for a favor. And when I needed him most, he let me down. I found out that he fired off a letter to Richard Schaffer of the City Planning Commission, stating his opposition to Riverside South. It gets worse. The guy then took a poll of West Side residents. How did they feel about Riverside South? If he backed the project, would they vote for him or not?

Obviously nabbing a few votes on the Upper West Side was more important to him than keeping my friendship. I know he has major regrets. While I can never forgive Andy for his lack of loyalty, he's actually a good guy. His father, Jerry Finklestein, is one of the great characters in New York. He is as solid as a rock, and a true friend. Andy's brother, Jimmy, runs the *New York Law Journal* and has always done an outstanding job. Andy, however, was under a lot of pressure at the time, and pressures make politics. He was running for mayor and in all honesty could not afford to alienate the West Side by voting for a Trump project. In the end, Andy got some very bad advice and he took it; I believe he wishes he had not. I believe he wishes he had gone the other way.

It's pointless to create a project of this scope—and go through with it—if it doesn't stimulate the economy. The construction industry in New York City was in a severe state of depression. New residential permits dropped from 12,079 in 1985 to 756 in 1989. One private office tower was under construction. I passionately wanted to turn it around. Riverside South will pump $2.5 billion into the economy over a five-year period. What more could I do for the city I adore?

Finally, after all of the years and all of the politicking, victory was at hand. The New York City Council voted 42–8 to approve the zoning on my job. Wonderful comments were made by (almost) all about the beauty and potential of this job. Accolades were thrown in every direction about how civic groups were able to come together and unite with a developer to build something that was appealing, responsible, and proper.

Unlike the Coliseum project and the many other halted projects that were litigated for years, this was a case where everyone came together. Richard Kahan, Dinkins, the civic leaders, and I all hoped that this would be used in the future as a yardstick for other development projects.

I had my vote, and I had my zoning, and now I could look for financing and partners. Before the zoning came through, of course no one was interested. Now everyone wanted to join with me. I had a suspicion I'd be taken to court by a few West Side residents, so when I was, there was no surprise. When a highly respected New York Supreme Court justice saw that the civics had teamed up with me, he saw how ludicrous the suit was. Seldom, he said, if ever, had he seen a developer joined by those people who are almost *always* on the other side of the equation. He immediately threw the case out of court.

In the most uncanny way, the Riverside South project follows a rule I try to live by: Get your zoning in a bad economic climate, and begin building in a good one. I got a little lucky. There could have been no worse climate than in the early 1990s, when I got my zoning. Frankly, I'm not sure that the zoning on this site would have been possible in good or even normal times. It was only the depressed state of New York and the country in general that allowed me to get what I wanted—the best deal possible.

As for always building in a booming economic climate: From the day I got that zoning, the market began to improve. People were flocking to me. Everyone wanted to finance the job or join up as a partner. After getting my final approvals, a frenzy of calls came in from potential investors and partners. Some were legit and some were not. One caller was a character named Danielli Bodini, who was at one time married to the grandaughter of the legendary Charlie Allen of Allen and Company. This guy worked with me for months trying to figure out every aspect of the job. He would wheel and deal with my people, talk joint venture all over the place. He seemed revved up to do a deal.

I had heard terrible things about him but really had no idea whether or not they were true. When you're doing deals and talking to many people, you want to try and keep an open mind. But you do want to keep your guard up, and I sure as hell did. I began hearing rumors that while he was talking to us in "a most friendly way" he was, behind my back, negotiating with Chase Manhattan Bank and the others to try to buy back my mortgage at a discount. Part of the mortgage was personally guaranteed, and I had no doubt, after hearing these rumors, that if he was able to get the mortgage, he would immediately foreclose on the project, call in my personal guarantee, and try to take total control.

I didn't let on that I was wise to what he was doing. He would come in all roly-poly with big smiles, while at the same time I suspected he was working very hard to screw me big time. I informed the bank that if it went along with this guy's idea, it could have a major liability. Even the bank did not seem to be happy with Bodini's antics. In the end, the only thing he did was to force me to hurry up in making my financing and partnership deal—I didn't want to give this guy even the slightest opening.

Despite all the offers, some of which were quite compelling, I decided to go with Hong Kong investors Henry Cheng of New World Development and Vincent Lo. Both men have become great friends, having placed confidence in me at a time when others weren't so sure. I'll never forget one morning, picking up *The New York Times* and reading a quote from Frankie Chang, who works with the group.

When asked why these Hong Kong investors had backed this project, he simply stated, "We made this investment for one reason. Donald Trump."

During the nasty and protracted zoning process, my mortgage loan with the Chase Manhattan Bank and its participants had gotten to be quite high, at one point in excess of $300 million. I had informed them that I would not be making interest payments.

The investors in what is currently called Riverside South (the name will be changed) are among the most sophisticated in the world. They came into the city at a low moment, and together we bought the mortgage back for a huge discount from Chase Manhattan Bank. We went to Chase together and bought what could have been considered to be about a $320 million mortgage, including all costs, for $82 million. Had the banks stayed in, they would have gotten all their money back and then some, but fortunately for us, it was not their decision to do so. Therefore, not only do we have beautiful, pristine, professional zoning on the finest large-scale piece of land in America, but we substantially reduced the costs I'd accumulated over the years. The bank wanted the money and did not want to wait years to get it. I don't blame them, but if they'd waited, they would have cashed out high. Henry Cheng and Vincent Lo could feel it too, despite being from the other side of the world. That's great instinct! They were willing to bet on me and New York City. Their bet has already paid off: We are under construction on almost $500 million worth of towers. My Hong Kong partners have always been enthusiastic and supportive of our partnership. I recently received the following note:

Dear Donald,
    I note that we have saved more than 4.6 millions in the sub-contract awards for our first two buildings up to last week. Accord-

ing to Ambrose and Paul, we couldn't have done so well without you taking charge in making the final award calls.

Your knowledge and connections with the local sub-trades are invaluable. Your personal involvement in this effect is much appreciated.

Thank you very much.

Best regards,
Henry Cheng

The West Side Railroad Yards is proving to be, after a long and arduous struggle, one of the greatest real estate deals ever. And as for my relationship with the civic groups—people who my advisors told me I should never even contemplate making a deal with—it's certainly blossomed. Richard Kahan has left the UDC chairmanship in order to run for governor; he was replaced by a terrific and dynamic guy named Phil Howard, who wrote the best-seller *The Death of Common Sense.* The collaboration has worked out so well that after our contract with them expired, we extended it for another ten years. They are terrific people and have had great impact on this development, an impact that will be seen and felt by millions of people for many years to come.

I want to conclude this chapter by describing a wonderful event that took place in 1995 right next to this project: the Nation's Day Parade. More than a million people participated and turned it into one of the biggest events in the history of New York City. I think it was a reaction to the Veterans Day Parade, which took place on Riverside South the year before, when our proud veterans marched up Riverside South into a virtual downpour. They could not have been a more unhappy lot. Fewer than a hundred people had watched the parade. These are the guys who really had the guts—they protected our freedom during World War I, World War II, the Korean War, the Vietnam War, and the Gulf War. No one cared. No one watched.

Traffic was out of control. Cars from side streets were driving right through the parade. Pedestrians didn't pay the slightest attention to our veterans.

The debacle was widely reported in the front pages of the New York *Daily News,* the *New York Post,* and *The New York Times.* While few people watched the parade, many watched the aftermath. The following day, I received a call from our great mayor of New York City, Rudy Giuliani, asking me whether or not it would be possible to meet with a group of veterans who wanted to do it differently the following year.

Rudy Giuliani has done an amazing job as the mayor of New York, helping to make the city a hot place—again. I told him that I would be glad to meet with these veterans. A small delegation came in, headed by James K. Kallstrom, a tremendous guy and the head of

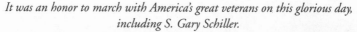

It was an honor to march with America's great veterans on this glorious day, including S. Gary Schiller.

Again, the Nation's Day Parade: An unlikely group. Governor Pataki and Lieutenant Governor Betsy McCaughey-Ross in the same picture? Senator D'Amato and Mayor Giuliani marching as well?

the New York office of the FBI. Jim told me that the last Veterans Day Parade was a complete disgrace, an embarrassment to the nation. They made it quite clear that they would like to do another parade. They asked me to lead it as Grand Marshal—essentially they wanted my stamp of approval. They needed dollars. They knew I could raise lots of money and get additional donors. They also knew I would attract a lot of press.

I agreed. I thought it would be fun, and I knew it was important. Mayor Giuliani was pledging the support of the city. I put up money; others matched it.

I always knew there was a military out there, but I had no idea such high quality people led it. This is something I got to know, and know very well, over the next few months. One of these people in par-

George and Libby Pataki. Two great people.

ticular, Admiral Bill Owens, who sat on the Joint Chiefs of Staff as the head of the Navy, became a very close friend of mine. Bill not only had that incredible look and demeanor, but he had a level of intelligence and a winning attitude that I would match against any of the top business leaders in this country. But more on Bill and the Joint Chiefs of Staff later.

At the City Hall press conference, it was becoming obvious to all that I and the others had done quite a job. The press was going absolutely crazy for the idea because they too knew what a shame the last Veterans Day Parade had been. There were many reporters and great spirit among them—a kind of spirit I never knew the media had. It turned out that the media, too, was proud of our great military heritage, and in particular our wonderful veterans. They could not have been nicer or more respectful toward what we were doing. Huge television newscasts were done on what was soon to take place. The military committed to having thousands of soldiers attend the parade and march. Grandstands were being set, and almost everybody invited, from the top politicians in the United States to the heads of the armed services and even, yes, many of my businessmen friends from New York, promised to attend. It actually got to a point where a lot of my civilian friends, some of the biggest names in the country, were calling me and asking if they could march in the parade. I told them yes, providing they would pay $10,000 each toward the effort.

The morning of the parade turned out to be magical. The weather was perfect and the parade started to form. Hours before parade time, it was obvious that millions of people would be attending. The New York City police did an incredible job, but they were helped by the military themselves. Defense Secretary William Perry, Governor Pataki, Mayor Giuliani, Senator D'Amato, Senator Moynihan, Lieutenant Governor Betsy McCaughey-Ross, and all of the top generals and admirals came from all over the country, and indeed from all over the world, to attend this great parade. As we marched up Fifth Avenue, the people were lined up ten and fifteen deep for miles, and they were going wild. I was walking in the front row with the various dignitaries when Governor George Pataki, one of the greatest governors that New York State has ever had, pushed me forward and said, "Donald, you deserve to go to the front of this parade all by yourself." I was embarrassed to actually do so, but appreciated the gesture.

We began the parade on Fifth Avenue at about 50th Street and marched right by some of my buildings, including, of course, Trump Tower, which was packed to the rafters with people hanging from all over it. The parade lasted all day, with huge numbers of soldiers, sailors, and airmen proudly marching in formation until they arrived at 86th Street and Fifth Avenue and the end; many actually circled back to watch the others march. It is estimated that at least 1.4

million people showed up for that parade, as opposed to less than 100 people the year before. I was given all sorts of commendations and awards for what I did, but that was nothing compared to the friends I made and would make because of my involvement. It very much reminded me of what I did ten years earlier with the Vietnam Veterans Day Parade, which also turned out to be a tremendous success. The difference was, while I was very much involved with the Vietnam parade and put up much of the money, over $1 million, to see that it was a success, I was not as front and center as I was with the Nation's Day Parade. I just felt that something had to be done after the disgrace of the year before.

About a month after the parade had ended and everybody was still feeling good, I received a call from Admiral Bill Owens, who asked if he could come to see me. When he arrived in my office, we shook hands and embraced, much as two soldiers would do after winning a battle. He told me he was representing the Joint Chiefs of Staff in a request that I go to Washington in the near future to have lunch with Secretary of Defense William Perry and the entire Joint Chiefs of Staff. He said this was something that is virtually never done; that on occasion individual members of the Joint Chiefs will have lunch with someone, but almost never as a unit. In fact, he said that he could not even remember such an event ever taking place. The Joint Chiefs wanted to honor me for what I had done with the Nation's Day Parade. Naturally, I was very excited and gave an immediate yes. When I arrived at the Pentagon, I was taken to what is called the war room and informed that few civilians have ever been allowed to see this room. Pictures were taken of me, Secretary Perry, and the entire Joint Chiefs of Staff, and during lunch, presentations were made. I have never seen so many three- and four-star generals in my life, nor have I seen people who were more impressive—and I've seen people who are pretty impressive.

As one-star generals would come in to introduce a subject on how the country defends itself, I would say, "How come you're only a one-star general?" One of the men I got to know during this session was the chairman of the Joint Chiefs of Staff, General John Shalikashvili. This is a powerful man, a man of great authority and bearing who, if I were casting a movie of what the Joint Chiefs of Staff should look and be like, I would choose to play the lead. Each one of the people gathered in the room possessed tremendous bearing and strength—equal to or greater than those with whom I work at the top levels of civilian life. I was a little surprised by this, to be honest, but boy, did it turn out to be a pleasant surprise. While we're out making our deals and having fun doing so, these guys are keeping an eye on the world and the country. They gave me a preview of the world's hot spots, and each time I would say, "Gee, that sounds like a problem," they would look at me and smile, with total assurance, and explain how that country could easily be handled in case of a problem. With these guys and our military capability, anybody wanting to mess around with us would be in serious trouble.

This was one of the first days where, from the moment I left New York, I totally turned off the phone. I did not want messages, I did not want anything from the outside world—I wanted to focus on what was going on. At the end of the day, I could not have been more impressed. It showed me a whole new dimension of the United States and what is going on to defend it. These are some of the greatest men I have ever had the privilege to meet and they were thankful to me because I did something to highlight the men they most respect—the veterans. I now have the greatest admiration for the military, but far more important, I know this country is being watched over by a brilliant and talented group.

Mano a mano with Andre the Giant, 7 foot 7 inches and 580 pounds.

THE PRESS AND
OTHER GERMS

ONE OF THE CURSES OF AMERICAN SOCIETY IS THE SIMPLE
act of shaking hands, and the more successful and famous one becomes, the worse this terrible custom seems to get. I happen to be a
clean-hands freak. I feel much better after I thoroughly wash my
hands, which I do as often as possible. Recent medical reports have
come out saying that colds and various other ailments are spread
through the act of shaking hands. I have no doubt about this.

Almost nothing bothers me more than sitting down for dinner at a beautiful restaurant and having a man you've just seen leaving the men's room, perhaps not even having washed his hands, spot you and run over to your table with a warm and friendly face, hand outstretched. You have a decision to make. Do you shake this total stranger's hand, or do you insult him by saying that you would rather not? I have done both, and nothing works. If you shake his hand, you then get up to rewash your hands and inevitably somebody else comes over to you to shake hands. If you don't shake his hand, he walks away with a long face, totally insulted, and bemoans for the rest of his life how that bastard Donald Trump would not shake his hand.

To me the only good thing about the act of shaking hands prior to eating is that I tend to eat less. For example, there is no way, after shaking someone's hand, that I would eat bread. Even walking down the street, as people rush up to shake my hand, I often wonder to myself, why? Why risk catching a cold?

The Japanese have it right. They stand slightly apart and do a quick, formal, and very beautiful bow in order to acknowledge each other's presence. This is an ancient act, and was probably originated eons ago by someone like me—a germ freak. Whoever formalized this greeting was very smart, and far beyond his time. I wish we would develop a similar greeting custom in America. In fact, I've often thought of taking out a series of newspaper ads encouraging the abolishment of the handshake. At the very least, people would realize why I hate to shake hands and not take it personally. In any event, if any of you folks reading this book really like me, please approach me at any time, in a restaurant or elsewhere, and don't stick out your hand but simply bow. I will bow back and greatly appreciate the thought.

Now, for another annoying subject: reporters. People of the media are often recklessly devious and deceptive. Recent polls have shown

BILL FITZ-PATRICK/OFFICIAL WHITE HOUSE PHOTOGRAPH/THE REAGAN LIBRARY

This is one hand I didn't mind shaking.

that the general public is wise to the act. Journalism—if you even want to call it that, these days—is widely considered one of the most untrustworthy professions in the United States.

I've always thought experience to be a double-edged sword—you evolve from it, but sometimes it hurts you. Only one thing is for sure: You always learn from it. And that's what matters. Only in the worst of times are you really tested. Unfortunately, during the time I was trying to turn my finances around, my life was further complicated by publicity. The tabloids and newspapers alike spill more ink on Donald Trump than, it seems, on almost anyone else. At the time, I was the poster boy for every newspaper and magazine in the country, business and otherwise.

Here's one rude example. I experienced a series of bizarre incidents with the editor of *The New Yorker,* Tina Brown. She is married to Harry Evans, the publisher of Random House, which is publishing this book. Therefore, I doubt this passage will be allowed to be printed, but if it is, you know that Harry Evans is, indeed, a man of

---

It was a pleasure meeting Gorbachev. But still, I hate shaking hands.

I made another exception for Mickey Mantle.

great courage and conviction. Tina Brown is a very respected editor, who was able to bring *Vanity Fair* to life, and has been trying, without much success, to do the same thing for *The New Yorker.*

I received a call from Tina asking whether or not it would be possible to have breakfast. "*The New Yorker* wants to profile you," she cooed in haughty British tones.

A week later we met at the Plaza Hotel. Tina was quite pleasant and charming, particularly when she brought up the subject of *The New Yorker* doing a major story on me. Honestly, I was reluctant to cooperate. To me, Tina's word was not so good. Sometime in the mid-1980s she had asked me to be profiled for *Vanity Fair* by an unattractive reporter named Marie Brenner. Tina had intimated to me that the story would be wonderful. Wrong. The story was, in fact, one of the worst ever written about me. I was furious at Tina for quite a while, but as the old cliché goes, time heals all wounds.

Set the calendar forward to 1997. Tina and I sit across from each other at breakfast at the Plaza Hotel. She's going on and on about how I am doing better than ever before. She insists the profile will be much better than the *Vanity Fair* article. There we sat, a decade hence, and Tina Brown was at it again, asking me to agree to a profile. She is a

Liberace was a great performer and a great man. We all miss him dearly.

very persuasive woman. She told me, "You will love the piece, you'll absolutely love it!"

After listening awhile, I agreed. I thought, how many editors call someone for breakfast in order to convince him to do a story that they could write without him anyway?

The next day I got a call from *The New Yorker*'s reporter, Mark Singer. When he came into the office, I immediately sensed that he was not much of anything, nondescript, with a faint wiseguy sneer and some kind of chip on his shoulder.

Singer reminded me a bit of Harry Hurt, a guy who wrote an inaccurate book about me. While Singer was slightly more physically attractive than Harry Hurt (which, by the way, wasn't difficult), Singer had *scar* written all over him. He kept trying to convince me that I would like the piece, and like a jerk, I kept believing him. I spent a lot of time with him, and in the end, this was what embarrassed me most—that I would give so much of myself to somebody who was only interested in doing a hatchet job.

When the piece came out, I absolutely hated it. At first I was very angry and wanted to immediately call or write Tina Brown. But I knew that if I did, it would end up being a big story and the magazine would start selling like crazy. So I decided to hold my venom until after that issue had disappeared from the newsstands.

As soon as the story came out, I got a call from Richard Johnson, the very clever *New York Post* reporter, who happens to head up the Page Six gossip column. Other reporters, likewise, called to ask my opinion of the story. Rather than saying I hated it, I called it the longest and most boring story I had ever read. So long and boring, in fact, that I never really got to finish it—and until recently, that was 100 percent true.

Eventually I also called one of the finest people I know, Steve Florio, the chief executive of Condé Nast and Tina Brown's boss. While he didn't seem particularly happy with what Singer had written, there was nothing he could do about it, nor would I ask Steve to do anything, anyway. But I decided to write a letter to Tina Brown, which I'll share with you here.

> Dear Tina:
>
> I guess the only good news about your recent story on me is that people don't seem to be reading *The New Yorker*. Almost nobody even mentioned it to me (unlike the two recent covers of *People* magazine).
>
> Obviously you are not making much of an impact despite all of the money you are spending at *The New Yorker*. The story was so long and boring that I found myself unable to take my eyes off the Knick game—and the story was about me! It is obvious that Mark Singer is a third-rate writer with a first-rate agenda.
>
> In any event, don't ever ask me to do another story. You said, "It will be great, you'll love it"—you lied!
>
> Sincerely,
> Donald J. Trump

The reason I write this story is not to convince you that the media is all bad—it isn't—but rather to relate some of the lessons I've learned. Someone who screws you once will do it again. Tina Brown told me years ago that the Marie Brenner story would be wonderful. It was not. Years later she told me that the Mark Singer story would be wonderful. It was not. I did not learn my lesson. As I stated in my letter, *The New Yorker* is a loser, and Tina Brown has done little, despite spending huge sums of money, to turn it around. *The New Yorker* has taken huge financial losses since Tina Brown took over and will continue to do so. Many people think the magazine was far better before Tina got there—and I am one of them. But she hit me once, and then she hit me again. This was not such an important event, in retrospect, but I should have learned my lesson. It will not happen a third time. There's been so much fuss about Tina Brown, and yet Graydon Carter, who replaced her as editor at *Vanity Fair,* has taken that magazine to new heights, far eclipsing what Brown had done. Perhaps Graydon should run *The New Yorker,* too.

Of all the writers who have written about me, probably none has been more vicious than Neil Barsky of *The Wall Street Journal.* He would come, look me in the eyes, smile, and then proceed to write the most malicious things. Often he wouldn't even call prior to writing a piece, and I would be shocked, the next day, to see what had been said. Neil Barsky had one thing going for him: the tremendous power and reputation of *The Wall Street Journal.*

In any event, during the course of my difficulties, Barsky was getting worse and worse. He was a pushy bastard, aggressive to an extreme, and obnoxious as could be. And, it turned out, he was just a little bit too greedy. I'll never forget the day that Nick Ribis walked into my office and said, "You won't believe this, but Neil Barsky has just asked for tickets to the Foreman/Holyfield fight." The heavyweight championship fight between George Foreman and Evander Holyfield was being staged that week at Trump Plaza in Atlantic City, and the tickets cost approximately $1,000 a piece. I couldn't believe that Barsky was asking for tickets. A short time later Nick came back to say that not only did Barsky ask for two tickets, but now he wanted a third, and perhaps a suite at the Taj Mahal. Ribis and I were stunned. "Give him the tickets," I said, "but the next time he writes anything I'm going to blast him like he never got blasted before."

Sure enough, it happened. Only a short time after the fight, Barsky was at it again. After he wrote a particularly vicious article, I said, "That's it." I reported his outrageous ticket requests to *The Wall Street Journal,* and it became a major story overnight. All over people were reading about *The Wall Street Journal* reporter who had asked for tickets to a fight.

An intrepid interviewer, Barbara Walters follows me to a construction site. She promised me she wouldn't mention my divorce if I went on her show. She did!

Initially, *The Wall Street Journal* tried to dampen the story by claiming that there was nothing wrong with Barsky getting a ticket to see a fight, in that he was covering the casino industry. However, when this *Journal* executive was informed by another newspaper reporter that Barsky had taken more than one ticket, he clearly became ruffled. He was definitely upset, and it wasn't playing well for Neil Barsky.

It is my opinion that, except for the exposure that *The Wall Street Journal* had, Neil Barsky would have been history. He stayed on at *The Wall Street Journal,* but he seemed to keep a lower profile for a long time. I have heard that Barsky is rated a world-class poker player, and perhaps he is. Well, he is a mean and cunning guy and certainly nobody's fool, but in this case he overplayed his hand.

As Barsky reportedly told a friend, "I gotta hand it to Donald Trump, that bastard—he went after me and fucked up my entire career." Likewise, I have to hand it to Neil Barsky. Despite this trauma, he has staged a magnificent comeback. He is now an analyst at Morgan Stanley, John Mack's firm, and probably making far more money than he did as a reporter. It sounds like he owes me big time.

The media is simply a business of distortion and lies. One of my biggest fears concerns how I'll be perceived after I'm gone. While I'm alive I can protect myself pretty well, but the fact is, even when I'm here, the press writes distorted and untruthful things about me almost daily. For example, books written by Harry Hurt and Jack O'Donnell, a disgruntled former employee I hardly even knew, were so off the mark that twenty-five or fifty years from now, if people use this crap as a backlog on me, it will be very unfair. These guys didn't know me, didn't like me, and only wanted to produce a really negative product. Stories they told about my life and business were seldom correct, nor did these authors want them to be. The good news is that nobody bought their garbage, and I was able to blunt the impact of the books' sales by publicly explaining the facts. This is why neither book was successful—I really knocked the shit out of both of them and took down their credibility. Unfortunately, when I'm not around, these books will be out there as references. I am asking the future writers of this world to pay little, if any, attention to the rubbish that's been written about me. It's unfair, untrue, and, generally speaking, very boring.

When I think of the media, I often think of politics—the two go hand in hand. For example, my experience with *The Village Voice*, Wayne Barrett specifically, has been terrible. They have so many preconceived notions about me, all of which are politically motivated. Barrett calls himself an investigative reporter. I think he's a jerk. However, unlike the media, politics is a business of relevance. People have always asked me if I'll ever be involved in politics. It seems every so often there's some unfounded rumor that I'm considering seeking office—sometimes even the presidency! The problem is, I think I'm too honest, and perhaps too controversial, to be a politician. I always say it like it is, and I'm not sure that a politician can do that, although I might just be able to get away with it because people tend to like me. Honesty causes controversy, and therefore, despite all the polls that say I should run, I would probably not be a very successful politician.

One of the great guys, Ted Turner, opening up his TNT network at Trump Plaza.

INVESTING:

CAVEAT EMPTOR

PERHAPS THE QUESTION I AM MOST OFTEN ASKED IS WHERE, when, and how should someone invest their money. My answer is usually a very quick and terse "Good luck." The reason for this is simple. If I recommend an investment and it turns out badly, it will be my fault. I will always be blamed. If, on the other hand, the investment turns out to be brilliant, earning tremendous amounts of money, people are quick to forget that it was I who made the recommendation in the first place. This, unfortunately, is human nature. It's how the game is played. If it's bad, you take the blame. If it's good, you get no credit. As I tell my young employees all the time, "Welcome to life."

But in this case I figure, What the hell, you folks are paying to buy this book, and I should at least give you some basic tips as to how you should invest your money. Just remember to give me all the credit and promise not to blame me! I've watched investments that I thought were sure bets go down the tubes, and I've watched what should have been terrible investments make tremendous fortunes for people. The truth is, you can never really predict, but you can at least give yourself a fighting chance.

I'm a great believer in two things: people and track records. There's an old expression on Wall Street: "It seems that it's always the same people who get lucky." The fact is, these people are "lucky" for various reasons. They do their research, have tremendous instincts and brainpower, and then there's the X factor—that special ingredient that enables people to make money. Some of them make money for themselves, some make money for others, and some do both.

Take Alan "Ace" Greenberg, the legendary head of Bear Stearns. Alan has always made a great deal of money for everyone, including himself. He is an amazingly streetwise guy with a tremendous intellect. He is a champion bridge player, and that is not by coincidence. Over the years, Alan has called me because he knows I spend time with a number of celebrities. Ace picks up the paper and reads that I'm out with Mike Tyson, Evander Holyfield, a host of rock stars, models, and actors. He always tells me that if I was a real friend to these celebrities, I would advise them to save their money, to be very conservative and very smart.

He watched what was happening to Mike Tyson in the newspapers. This was a number of years ago, before Mike's problems and prison term. Ace saw that Mike's money was going fast and furious, so he called me to offer to watch over Mike's money, as he does for many others, and to ask that I please tell Mike to give him a call. Ace wanted no money for this guardianship; he just felt sorry for the many athletes and stars who lose all of their money to incompetent or dishonest managers. In the most emphatic tones, I told Mike to contact Ace, but he never called. Money is just not that important to him. I'm not sure that he even cares about it. In any event, Mike has gone through millions; hopefully, he'll always have plenty left.

I am friendly with so many athletes, musicians, and entertainers who have been ripped off—big league—by their managers. These people often reach the highest peak of their professions, thinking they're building a major nest egg. They trust too much, only to find out that their money has been stolen or, more often than not, poorly invested, and they are left with nothing. A very sad case is one of the greatest basketball players of all time, Kareem Abdul-Jabbar. After years of playing in the NBA, taking in millions of dollars, Abdul-Jabbar found that he had suffered huge investment losses. Abdul-Jabbar blamed his manager. The manager admitted some "bookkeeping irregularities," but denied the losses were his fault. Whoever was at fault, the net result was that Abdul-Jabbar had to play a couple more years.

This should serve as an important lesson to stars and civilians alike. Have checks and balances. Don't trust your "manager," no matter how competent and trustworthy he may seem. Be especially wary if this person is somehow related to you or your spouse. Some of the biggest horror stories I have heard are when the money is managed by a brother, a parent, a cousin—even a husband or wife. If you're related to your manager, you often drop your guard. If you're not related, keep in mind that some of the most evil and deceptive people are the ones with the smoothest tones and the most sophisticated style. They can talk you in or out of anything, quickly and effectively.

With Adnan Kashoggi—one of the greatest dealmakers of all time.

Great investment advice is sometimes costly and sometimes not. Either way, always take a look at the investment manager's track record. Whether the person is a professional or a friend, find out how well he did, year by year, for as far back as you can. If the manager is a professional, get hold of some of the many newsletters published each month rating the various funds and fund managers. Try to at least get five-year histories.

There are many great investments to be made, but some industries just seem better than others. Today the computer and technology industries are hot, but that doesn't mean that they won't cool off quickly. I know nothing about these industries, but it just seems to me that they are overheated, and competition is strong. When I read about all of the different companies producing new and varied forms of computers and bringing them out by the thousands, it seems like a very tough business to me. But then, I don't even know how to turn on a computer. Therefore, I'm not a natural investor in technology. If you are drawn to this sector, at least approach it with an advisor.

The problem with investing in any one industry is that an industry can turn from good to bad overnight. That's why mutual funds are not bad investment ideas; they vary their portfolios and invest in different segments of the economy. You don't get the biggest hit this way—for instance, it's not as good as investing in the single hot stock—but it does reduce your risk of failure and negativity.

Today I am very concerned about the stock market. You ask yourself, how high can it go? There are pockets of strength and pockets of weakness, but in general, you can't help but wonder when it will crash. The one thing we know for sure, without question, is that the market *will* go down, and probably very severely. It's really a question of time—will it be now, next year, or five years from now? History shows a constant and consistent wave of ups and downs. Sometimes the wave is longer and higher and sometimes it is shorter and lower, but there is always a wave. The problem is, the market may keep soaring and then suddenly plummet. These movements are nearly impossible to predict. So when do you get in? And when do you get out?

I have often said that the stock market is the biggest casino of them all. The great gambler, who studies the odds, can often beat the house. With investing in the stock market, so many variables come into play. For instance, how much money do you have? Are you liquid or illiquid? The most important aspect of all: In gambling, you rely on yourself only; when investing in the markets, you have to be willing to rely on others.

I am a great believer in the power of real estate, but investing in real estate takes time, patience, knowledge, and instinct. Real estate is often at its best when it's leveraged, sometimes hugely leveraged, but that is a very risky proposition for people who are not fully aware of what they're doing. It's great to buy a building like 40 Wall Street for a very small amount—a seventy-two-story building for $1 million—fix it up, make it magnificent again, rent it, and mortgage the building for far more than you ever put into it in the first place. Reaping hundreds of millions of dollars in gain on an investment of just a million dollars, in a short time, is incredibly tough to do even during a bull market. But it also takes courage, conviction, and knowledge.

On a smaller scale, I have watched people buy houses that they thought were in a good location and had potential to be renovated. I have seen them work very hard over a period of months to make the houses beautiful again and sell them at a great profit. This is not a new idea, but it can be carried to much greater lengths.

Jerry Speyer, Goldman Sachs, David Rockefeller, and others, in a brilliant move, bought Rockefeller Center from the Japanese for a song. They are in the process of creatively fixing it up and making it a special place again. I predict they will reap huge profits for their endeavors.

For those who wish to invest in real estate but don't really have the knowledge, capital, patience, or time, I would suggest, but very cautiously, investing in one of the many REITs, Real Estate Investment Trusts, that are traded publicly and available to the public. Please be careful, however, because some of these REITs are getting overzealous. Their managers seem to want to buy anything in sight. Study the management, study the track records, and see how well they have done. If the track record is good, over a long period of time, you can almost bank on their success. If it isn't, please stay clear.

The chosen few can just go with their gut. Some of the greatest investors I have ever known invest by instinct, rather than research, study, or hard work. They just have a feeling that something is going to turn out well. If you look back over history, this is the way the greatest fortunes have been built. People had ideas that they truly believed in, and sometimes others laughed at them as they pursued their goals. Great and powerful companies were started by someone's mere instincts—often against all odds. Unfortunately, it is unlikely that most of the people reading this book will have that instinct. That

One of my first allies in Palm Beach—a great lady,
Estée Lauder.

ANGELIKA RINNHOFER

"Mr. Lebed, I ask you, how about the Trump International Casino on Red Square?"

is handed out to very few. It is a very special trait. What you can do, however, is invest with others who do have it. Again, go back to the track record.

There are so many funds today, with so many unbelievably talented people running them, that to not use this brainpower would be almost foolish. I played golf with a gentleman recently who is a top investor at one of the world's first-rank funds. I asked him how he was doing, even though I already knew the answer—he was doing great. He is a brilliant guy who actually believes that it makes very little difference whether the markets go up or down for him to make money. He has so many different guards and safeties, known as hedges, that if he is investing on the upside when the market goes down, he tells me (although I find it hard to believe) he still comes out ahead. Some of his theories are pretty far out and very complex. He uses formulas that nuclear physicists wouldn't understand. I actually like to keep it a little more simple, and I don't believe that you can fully guard against catastrophe. Nevertheless, I'd rather have my money with a guy like this, who has a long history of success and truly believes he is guarding against the downside, than put my money with somebody who, in all likelihood, doesn't know what he is doing.

This has been a very unusual time in the history of the stock market. The major company stocks like GE, IBM, General Motors, Ford, and Exxon have gone up far more than the stocks of the smaller companies, even the smaller well-run companies, despite how well the smaller companies have done. It's probably the first time in history that this has happened, when putting your money into these so-called safer companies has given you far greater returns than if you hit big on a small, aggressive, and far more risky company. This has been great for the American public and more. Tremendous amounts of money are being made by people who just wanted to preserve their capital. How would you like to be investing in GE, for instance, and watch your stock double, and then double again, in a very short period? It's really fantastic for everyone, and in particular guys like me who build and often sell real estate to the people who are making fortunes in the stock market.

There are so many different forms of investments and so many different personal situations that it's very hard to give advice appropriate to everyone. Huge amounts of money will be made and lost over the coming years. Don't let yours be lost. Be smart, be tough, keep your guard up, and study. Use the best people possible to guard over your future, and don't ever put yourself in a position where you are risking it all. Watch for the downside, and the upside will take care of itself.

TRUMP COLLECTION/DAVIDOFF STUDIOS

The poster boy for fighting back. My friend Sylvester Stallone strikes one of his famous Rocky Balboa poses.

DEALING:

A WEEK IN THE LIFE OF THE COMEBACK

TRUMP: THE ART OF THE DEAL WAS ONE OF THE BEST-selling business books of all time and was, along with *Bonfire of the Vanities,* the best-selling book of 1988. Random House, my publisher, could not have been happier, and I could not have had more fun or pleasure from this great success. In that book was a chapter called "Dealing: A Week in the Life." For some reason, that chapter seemed to be one of the most popular in the book, so I thought I would bring my

"Week in the Life" into the 1990s, an interesting period because it included far and away the worst depression since 1929, followed shortly thereafter—*now*—by what is probably the strongest economic time in our country's history, even stronger than the wild and woolly 1980s.

Hence, as you can imagine, I've had two types of weeks during the 1990s. The first type was a very negative one, in the early part of the decade when I was fighting for survival. These weeks consisted of twenty-four-hour workdays, unending meetings, conferences, and phone calls, with almost no time to do anything but work. Ranting and raving, cajoling, always selling, and generally having to be either the nicest guy in the world or one of the worst, I ended up getting my way and coming out far stronger, in the end, than I ever was in the 1980s.

I consider the early part of the 1990s to be my most brilliant period. This is the time when my abilities showed the greatest in that I was under tremendous pressure to perform in an economy that had totally collapsed. I won't describe a week in the life of the early 1990s because some of the things I did then, the methods I used, the screaming, shouting, and foul language, I wouldn't feel comfortable putting in writing.

Today is a far more pleasant period, and I'm delighted to give a semblance of what a week in my life is like.

Monday

5:30 A.M.   I normally wake up at this hour—and never to an alarm clock. I never drink coffee—only Diet Coke. I read *The New York Times, The Wall Street Journal,* the New York *Daily News* and the *New York Post.*

9:00 A.M.   I take the elevator to my Trump Tower office. My first call is to Andy Stone and Bill Adamski, two of the most brilliant guys on Wall Street, who invest huge amounts of money for First Boston

Credit Suisse, and have become major players in the real estate markets in New York and beyond. These guys were the first ones to realize the potential of downtown Manhattan and perhaps have more new money wisely invested downtown than anybody else. This investment, as like most investments they have made, has paid off handsomely. I talk to them about possibly financing the St. Moritz Hotel on Central Park South, which I am tearing down to make way for a superluxury condominium tower. They have great interest in both projects.

9:30 A.M.   An Argentinean developer comes to see me along with Abe Wallach and Andy Weiss, my heads of Real Estate and Construction, respectively. The Argentinean wants to build a Trump Tower in Buenos Aires, using my name to sell apartments and using my skills of conception and design in order to get the product that could be sold for the highest prices in Argentina. He is a good developer, and perhaps we will go forward, but the chances are better than not that we won't.

Many people have come to me over the last couple of years wanting to use the Trump name in some form, on a building in order to capitalize on the cachet. I, on the other hand, have not been easy. It is very important that the building be the best in the city or country, or my franchise would go downhill very quickly. In every case I have turned the various developers or institutions down, but at some point, when the quality improves, I will be doing something like this.

10:30 A.M.   Binky Urban comes in to see me. She is the very talented literary agent representing me on my book, and she lets me know there is great interest from publishing houses in doing a third number-one best-seller (it better be!). She tells me where we stand, and I tell her to go ahead. My first choice is Random House because they did such a great job on my first two books, especially *Trump: Surviving at the Top*. The last thing I wanted to be doing at that time in my life was a book, and it still went to number one on the lists. Binky thinks this can be the biggest of them all, and I can only tell you I have worked hard on it, even harder than I did on *Trump: The Art of the Deal.*

During both these meetings as always, I receive many phone calls, too numerous to list, on various different topics ranging from Miss Universe to Riverside South. It is truly a wild and maddening scene— but fun!

11:15 A.M. I speak to Howard Stern about the premiere of his movie. Howard is an amazing guy, much different in person than on the air. On the air he is wild and crazy but totally brilliant. He talks for hours, practically without notes, about subjects as varied as you can get but mostly about sex. His ratings are through the roof; his is by far the number-one show in New York. He has become a true phenomenon within the industry itself. His movie, *Private Parts,* has just come out, and for a couple of weeks it is the number-one movie in the country. He likes to call himself the King of All Media—and he is not wrong. His opening was amazing—a total hoot. Thousands of people lined the streets outside the theater. Howard is unique, a really nice guy, and he has one of the nicest wives of anyone I know, Alison. My only disagreement with Howard is the way he treats Frank and Kathie Lee Gifford, two great people I have known for a long time. I constantly tell Howard, "Stop already," but he just won't.

11:30 A.M. I call Bruce Turner, the gaming analyst for Salomon Brothers, the investment-banking house. Bruce has had a hard time of it lately. He had been touting Las Vegas, and the casinos just announced their worst June in ten years. Circus Circus, the Mirage, and other stocks he liked are way down. According to most experts there is just too much capacity coming on in Las Vegas, and some companies will get absolutely killed. He can't back away from his earlier predictions, or he'll be saying to the analyst community that he was

My good friends Frank and Kathie Lee Gifford.
These two unfortunately understand just how vicious the press can be.

wrong. I'm trying to get Bruce to back Trump Hotels & Casino Resorts, but it's like talking to a brick wall.

12:00 P.M.   I go to the new Nike store at Trump Tower, where I meet with Phil Knight. Phil is twenty years ahead of everyone else in retailing. What he's done with Nike is incredible. The new store, right next to Tiffany's on Fifty-seventh Street, adjoining Trump Tower, is one of the most successful in New York, and we talk about the big ribbon cutting with Tiger Woods, Patrick Ewing, and many other great ath-

At Howard Stern's birthday party.

letes. I don't usually eat lunch, I grab something on the fly. I love red meat.

1:15 P.M.   I see Eddie Malloy, the head of the New York Building and Construction Trades Council and a man I always enjoy being with. I call Eddie "Angel Eyes" because he has the most beautiful blue eyes you've ever seen, yet under those blue eyes is one of the roughest, toughest guys you'll ever meet—and also one of the nicest. Eddie is constantly pushing jobs in New York and looking to get buildings built, the bigger the better, so his men can be employed. Years ago, when I was trying to get the zoning on the West Side Railroad Yards, Eddie Malloy and a group of top labor leaders were always present to try and push the politicians into giving me what I wanted. I didn't even know him then, but he fought just as hard as if I were his best friend. Eddie is loved by his men and women and respected by everyone.

2:30 P.M.   Ken Moelis and Joe Roby, two of my favorite investment bankers, come into my office. They did a terrific job taking my casinos public last summer. Once a financial reporter asked me for ideas for a story, and I told him, "Write a story on Joe Roby." One of the most powerful and respected men on Wall Street, he's a man that very few people know—Joe wants it that way. He is a quiet, brilliant guy who runs one of the best organizations anywhere, Donaldson, Lufkin & Jenrette. Ken is a dealmaker par excellence. He led my public offerings through a highly technical and complicated maze of obstacles and did it with style and class. These are two great guys, and I could not have picked a better firm to represent me.

3:00 P.M.   Tom Barrack of Colony Capital calls. He is talking about buying the Mayfair Regent Hotel on Park Avenue and Sixty-fifth Street and wants my opinion. Tom is actually one guy who doesn't need many opinions from anyone. He is always at the beginning of the curve and sees things years before other people have any idea what's happening. We would later go on to develop the Mayfair Regent together as a superluxury condominium apartment house—and a big success.

3:30 P.M.   Peter Lynch of Fidelity arrives. He is a really unusual guy, and probably no one has done a better job at picking stocks and markets. He has become a friend of mine, but I think he likes me more for the fact that I help his charity, the Inner-City Scholarship Fund in Boston, than for anything else. Peter will ask me a large scale question like "What do you see for the real estate markets in the United States or New York?" then sit back and let me talk. It all goes into the very brilliant computer that is his brain, and after talking to me and probably lots of other folks, he forms ideas as to where we're all going—and those ideas always seem to be right.

4:00 P.M. I have a quick meeting with the folks who orchestrated the festivities and ribbon-cutting ceremony of Trump International Hotel and Tower. They want to discuss various upcoming events at Jean-Georges, restaurant.

5:00 P.M. Lots of calls are being taken and various people are on hold when I'm told that Richard Saltzman of Merrill Lynch has just come to the office. I really relate to Richard because not so many years ago, during my dealings with Merrill, he was a young, low-ranking employee I saw at meetings, but now he has risen practically to the top. He is respected by everybody and has made excellent decisions. I get a great thrill out of seeing a young man rise so quickly to a position of great power.

6:00 P.M. My daughter Ivanka calls. CBS wants Ivanka to host the Miss Teen USA pageant. She's never done live television, but she's definitely got what it takes. I tell Ivanka what CBS would like, and her reaction is mixed. She's become a very successful model, working with Monique Pillard and John Casablancas at Elite, and the question is whether or not doing the teen contest is in a totally different sphere than the modeling. She'll do whatever I ask her to do, but I really want the decision to be hers. It's a lot of pressure for a fifteen-year-old, especially when a lot of the girls in the pageant will be seventeen or eighteen—a big difference at that time in life. Ivanka ultimately decides to do the contest and works really hard with Maureen Reidy, the fantastic president of Miss Universe, in order to make sure everything goes well. Ivanka does a wonderful job, and the ratings are sky high. CBS is very happy.

I take various other phone calls and then go up to my apartment in Trump Tower. It is so serene and peaceful until the phones start ringing again. The workday never really ends.

Tuesday

9:00 A.M.   All morning long I have been on the phone with people about various deals. I like to call my kids in the morning to make sure they're fine. I believe they look forward to getting those calls.

Percy Pyne comes to see me, relevant to 40 Wall Street. He is the attorney representing the Hinnebergs, and we brainstorm about future deals and reminisce about our success with 40 Wall Street.

9:30 A.M.   We have a board meeting of Trump Hotels & Casino Resorts. Our board is composed of Pete Ryan, former chief financial officer of Chase Manhattan Bank, Nick Ribis, and me. The meetings are always interesting and fun. We are three smart men who work hard and take our position on this board seriously. We are loaded up with cash and have a wonderful cash flow, but we are constantly amazed that the stock price doesn't seem to be commensurate with the value of the company. We all know that someday it will be.

10:45 A.M.   Abe Wallach comes in with H. C. Lee of Hysan Development in Hong Kong. Mr. Lee and his wife are fabulous people who have purchased a number of apartments at Trump International. We are very proud to have them.

11:00 A.M.   A German television crew comes to my office for a quick interview. It will be part of a major piece on me that they're producing.

11:30 A.M.   I speak to Ethan Penner, the head of Nomura Securities, who has become a leader in finance on Wall Street. Ethan has decided, from what I understand, to move his offices. We talk about this, among other things. He is a truly dynamic guy, and Nomura must be very happy with the great job Ethan has done.

11:45 A.M.   I see Ron Perelman, a good friend and the owner of Revlon and many other companies. Ron is a great guy with incredible deal-making skills and instincts. He can be very tough, but inside he's really a pussycat. Ron and I talk 95 percent women and 5 percent deals.

12:00 P.M.   Bob Small arrives at the office, and we discuss the building of superluxury condominiums on the top two floors of the Plaza Hotel. Bob loves the idea, and so do I. It will make a lot of money and really add something to the Plaza. Bob is very committed to the project and to keeping Fairmont Hotel Company at the top of the curve, where he has brought it.

12:30 P.M.   Celine Dion's people call. She is scheduled to perform at Mar-a-Lago, my Palm Beach club, and they want to clear up a few last-minute details. Celine is a great talent, and everybody at Mar-a-Lago is looking forward to her show that Saturday night. The place is going to be packed, and my biggest problem is having to turn down almost everybody who wants to attend. Ultimately, her performance goes off without a hitch, and everybody is amazed at the beauty of her voice.

12:45 P.M.   I go to a studio to do a video conference. They have paid me a lot of money just to use my voice. It takes approximately ten minutes, and I'm out. The commercial is to run for a long time, and later many people would tell me they heard my voice on it. I guess it wound up being quite successful, because the company ultimately offered to pay additional money to extend its running period.

1:30 P.M.   I get a call from Les Moonves, the man who is working so hard to make CBS the number-one network. We joke around about how crazy the situation was at the Grammys. I didn't get the right set of tickets.

2:00 P.M.   People from B'nai B'rith come in. I have agreed to give a speech to their organization that night at a major hotel. They tell me the place is going to be packed, and they want to go over what

I'll be saying. I tell them I really couldn't tell them what I'll be saying because I haven't given the speech any thought yet, but that I will start thinking about it—approximately five minutes before I speak!

4:00 P.M.   My friend Sylvester Stallone calls. Sly is really smart. For a long time his many assets were questioned, but now people know that whatever this guy wants to do, he just seems to be able to do. When it comes to Hollywood, he, Arnold Schwarzenegger, Bruce Willis, and a few others are in a class by themselves. Sly wants to play golf, so we agree to meet on Saturday morning at Winged Foot.

4:15 P.M.   Senator Bob Torricelli of New Jersey comes to my office looking for political support. He has been a friend of mine for a long time, and he is a truly effective guy. I ask him why he even bothered to come up—all he had to do was call. He thought it was the polite thing to do. I agree to help him, and I will continue to do so well into the future. We are lucky to have guys like Bob Torricelli representing the country. After all, he won one of the nastiest elections I have ever witnessed—and he won easily. He will be around for a long time and will do a great job.

5:30 P.M.   I get a call from Henry Cheng of New World, one of the largest developers in China. Henry and I, along with five other large Hong Kong–based companies, are building the huge West Side Railroad Yards development together, and he tells me how happy he is with the way things are going. We are ahead of schedule and very much under budget.

6:00 P.M.   I go to the apartment, make more phone calls, and then head over to the Grand Hyatt Hotel, where B'nai B'rith is waiting. I make my speech before a large crowd, and it goes well. I go back to Trump Tower, call the kids, and then just plain relax.

Wednesday

8:00 A.M.   I fly with my son, Eric, to a school he is thinking of attending. I have a great time being with him all alone, with no phone calls.

11:00 A.M.   I arrive back at the office and take a lot of calls—I'm swamped because of the four hours of office time I've missed. I try to make up for it.

12:00 P.M.   Richard Fields comes into my office. Richard is a fantastic guy; his wife, Meeka, is one of the most beautiful women I have ever seen. Richard is fighting for me on a number of fronts, but in particular he has led my campaign against casino gambling in New York State. He does a great job, and ultimately the measure fails. Gambling would've been a very bad thing for New York, and the politicians ultimately realized that. Richard, in my opinion, has a really great future.

1:30 P.M.   Arthur Caliandro comes to see me. He is the minister of Marble Collegiate Church, and a very popular one indeed. He has property where leases are coming due and wants my advice. I always give advice to Arthur, as I did to Dr. Norman Vincent Peale before him. We have made some great real estate deals together for the church.

2:00 P.M.   I get a call from one of my favorite people, Karl Malone, the great Utah Jazz basketball player. He is married to a really good woman, Kay, and he is sort of a fan of mine, I guess, as much as I am of his. He loves to ask me financial questions and also would like some advice on his contract, which is coming up for renewal. He was just voted the MVP of the NBA, barely beating out Michael Jordan, and he is very proud to have won that impressive honor. He is a great guy with an amazing physical presence. At six foot three, I am taller than most people, but when I stand next to the Mailman, I don't feel so big anymore. He towers over everybody.

4:00 P.M.   Bud Paxson, the head of Paxson Broadcasting, comes by
my office to say hello. We are friends from Palm Beach, and his terrific and beautiful wife also has the name Marla. They have a gorgeous
yacht, which he calls *Marla,* and everybody thinks it's mine. Bud and
I joke about it all the time, and I tell him, "It's great to have everybody
think you have this fantastic yacht and you don't have to pay for it."
Bud has done an amazing job with Paxson Broadcasting, making it

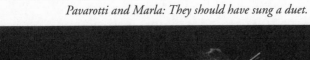

Pavarotti and Marla: They should have sung a duet.

one of the leaders in the entertainment industry in just a short period. Marla and he are members of the Mar-a-Lago club, and I am proud to have them both.

Julio Iglesias calls. He's scheduled to perform next month at Mar-a-Lago, and he wants to know if there are any particular songs I would like to hear. I tell Julio anything he sings is all right with me because he can make even the worst of songs sound great. His performance was flawless, as usual.

5:00 P.M.   I see Tommy Mottola, the head of Sony Records, who has catapulted that company to a position that is absolutely unbelievable. Tommy wants an apartment in one of my buildings, so we work out a deal. I love having people like Tommy with me—it's the ultimate recognition of what I build.

5:30 P.M.   Robert Earl comes to my office. Robert and Keith Barish are the impresarios of Planet Hollywood. We discuss the incredible success of their new All-Star Café at the Taj Mahal.

6:30 P.M.   I leave the office and go to my apartment. Marla is waiting for me with dinner, and while I really appreciate it, I realize that this is a marriage coming to an end. It just doesn't seem to be working out. Maybe it's my schedule, and probably it's my fault. But you've just got to really look forward to going home, and if you don't, something is critically wrong.

Thursday
9:00 A.M.   I have agreed with Lisa Belzberg Bronfman to be principal for a day. This honor has been shared by many major celebrities, such as Jane Pauley, Tipper Gore, Johnnie Cochran, and Bill Cosby, but for some reason (and as usual) the press seems to be following me. I go to P.S. 70 and have a wonderful time with the kids. I make a speech that everybody who was there loved, but unfortunately, *The*

New York Times wrote a slightly different version from what I'd delivered. In speaking before about five hundred young boys and girls, I talked strongly about working hard and incentives. When the *Times* story came out, it made me sound quite materialistic, which I guess I am. But it really failed to capture the flavor of the whole day. It also stated that I offered the children sneakers, rather than scholarships. I was really set up on this one, but what the hell, life goes on. I was very impressed with the principal, Mrs. Simon, and the way the school was run. The New York City school system does not get its just due for the great job it's doing. Rudy Crew, the chancellor, has had a great impact on the schools. And, working closely with Rudy Giuliani, the schools, as well as New York City itself, are really starting to click. Anyway, the honorary position should really be called "principal for a half day," because I was finished by about twelve-thirty.

12:30 P.M.   I go to lunch at the Four Seasons with Steve Florio of Condé Nast. Steve is a rough-and-tumble guy who has done an absolutely superb job bringing together the many pieces of Condé Nast to form a well-oiled machine. Steve and I are in different worlds, but we just like each other, and I have great respect and admiration for him. His boss, Si Newhouse, is one of the smartest, shrewdest (and nicest!) guys in New York, or anywhere else for that matter.

2:30 P.M.   Congressman Joe Kennedy comes to my office. He is probably going to run for governor of Massachusetts. I have known Joe for a long time, but he is taking a tremendous amount of heat over the situation with his first wife. She really went after him big league and certainly has left an imprint. He's a good guy, and I hope he makes it.

4:00 P.M.   I meet some of my lawyers regarding my will. My estate is very complex, and there aren't a lot of people who understand it, so I figure I might as well do it, because at least I do. Lawyers can really

Oh, that's Kissinger and me walking off the plane after a serious discussion of geopolitical security. He hung on my every word.

In Hollywood, Spielberg is in a class by himself.

screw things up if they're not properly watched. As I have often said, lawyers are usually only as good as their client.

4:30 P.M.   Nat Leventhal comes to my office to ask for help with Lincoln Center, which he has run for the last nine years. He has done extremely well. Lincoln Center has become a hot place in town and has really taken off under Nat's guidance. I agree to help.

5:00 P.M.   I meet with Charlie Reiss and Andy Weiss about Trump International Hotel and Tower. We're just about finished with the construction, and we've come in ahead of schedule and under budget. GE is really happy.

The guy who beat me out to play the role of Gordon Gekko in Oliver Stone's
Wall Street. *And you know what else? Greed is good!*

Friday

8:00 A.M.   I get a call from Peter Kalikow and Dan Cremins, two great friends of mine and very big factors in New York City real estate. Peter is being honored by New York Hospital on Monday and would like me to be there. I say absolutely yes.

8:30 A.M.   Terry Botwick from CBS arrives at my office. Terry is a young executive who is highly respected within the ranks of CBS and is going all the way. He is in charge of the Miss Universe contest, and we are discussing where we'll host next year's pageant for Miss Universe and Miss USA. I have a great deal of confidence in Terry's abilities.

8:45 A.M.   I call chairman Kyung Hoon Lee of Daiwoo, my new partner in the large and beautiful building we will soon begin opposite the United Nations, to be called the Trump World Tower. We are both very excited about this project.

9:00 A.M.   Carrie Chiang of the Corcoran Group comes to my office. Carrie is a terrific broker and sold 120 apartments at Trump Palace. She is now very much involved at both 610 Park Avenue and Trump International Hotel and Tower. She wants to know what I'm doing at the United Nations site, and I give a brief description. She is very excited.

9:15 A.M.   I go to the Plaza Hotel, where I make a speech to the Young Presidents Organization, or YPO as it is affectionately known. The place is totally packed; it's one of the largest crowds they've ever had. I am really happy to see this—it's just another column on the scorecard.

10:30 A.M.   I leave the Plaza and go to the Bankers Trust headquarters in lower Manhattan, where I meet with Frank Newman. Frank has come in and done an unbelievable job turning around Bankers Trust. He is one of the smartest and best respected bankers in the country. I look forward to working with Frank and Bankers Trust for years to come.

11:05 A.M.   I call Jason Ader, the gaming analyst for Bear Stearns. Jason is a smart young man who works very hard, and I think he's starting to like Trump Hotels.

12:00 P.M.   I have lunch with my good friend Dale Frey from GE. Often going to lunch is far from a treat for me, but I have always enjoyed being with Dale, and it's always instructive. He's a tough cookie, but underneath that toughness he's one of the nicest guys you'll ever meet—and very, very smart.

1:30 P.M.   Geraldo Rivera comes to my office. His show covers a wide range of topics, and I guess I'm to be one of them. He asks me about marriage, business, deals, everything under the sun in ten minutes or less. It's a lot of fun. Geraldo's a good guy.

2:30 P.M.   I meet with Bill Mack of Apollo and Steve Ross of Related about potential financings. These two guys are great friends and major forces in real estate and finance in general. Along with Leon Black, who heads Apollo, Bill has done a tremendous job. Steve Ross is like me—he just keeps going. He's doing jobs in West Palm Beach and all over the country, and knowing Steve, they'll all turn out to be successful.

2:45 P.M.   I call Joe Manganello of Bankers Trust just to say hello. Joe was one of the bankers who backed me and believed in me during the bad times. He is also, pure and simple, a great banker. I love him.

3:00 P.M.   I receive a phone call from Wayne Newton. As you probably know, Wayne had some major financial problems, and he called me and I gave him some very good advice. Now he goes around telling everybody how much I helped him, and I really appreciate that. He often starts shows by saying what a good guy I am. Well, Wayne is also a good guy. But I will say this: He is a much better entertainer than he is a businessman, and I don't think he'd be upset if he heard that. He's one of the best entertainers around, and I am trying to convince him that that's what he should be doing. He should sock away plenty of money, not invest it unwisely.

3:30 P.M.   I quickly go over to Jean Georges. I have rarely seen such professionalism. I am meeting with Peter Newcomb, the editor at *Forbes* magazine, who runs the Forbes 500. He tells me I was listed at $400 million last year. This year I'm valued at over $2 billion.

4:00 P.M.   Ben Lambert of Eastdil Realty calls. He has probably done better than any other real estate broker/consultant over the last number of years. He sits on the board of Hilton Hotels and is totally respected by both Steve Bollenbach and Barron Hilton. He is a terrific guy. We are working on a deal together.

5:00 P.M.   I see Len Riggio, the owner and president of Barnes & Noble Bookstores. Len has taken bookselling to new levels and has an imagination for the retailing process that few in his industry have even come close to. Barnes & Noble has become a major force in New York and throughout the country, and it is really all due to the knowledge, hard work, and genius of Len Riggio. I'm trying to get him to occupy a space I have, but he drives a hard bargain and I will probably be unsuccessful.

5:30 P.M.   Tom Bennison, president of Club Corporation of America, comes to see me. We are discussing doing a joint venture on various clubs. I have come to like Tom a lot. I wouldn't be surprised if something does happen.

It's getting late, and now I have to run to my plane to go and witness what will become one of the most controversial fights in the history of boxing—Mike Tyson versus Evander Holyfield. I look forward to the flight to Las Vegas, and the folks at the MGM Grand, Kirk Kerkorian, Alex Yemenidjin, and Terry Lanni, treat me terrifically, every bit as well as my own casinos do. The fight is an amazing event and beautifully executed. Unfortunately, Mike gets hungry and bites off a piece of Evander's ear. Everyone in the arena is shocked, but what the hell can you do? It's just another week in the life of Donald Trump!

J. J. RAYMAN (ALL RIGHTS RESERVED)

In order to come back you've got to have a champion's heart.
I never stopped believing in the Yankees. This is a charity event
at Yankee Stadium.

INGREDIENTS FOR SUCCESS

THERE IS AN OLD SAYING THAT IF YOU PUT A LOT INTO
something, chances are, you will get a lot out of it. While there's
nothing fancy or pretty about it, plain old hard work is, with very few
exceptions, a primary ingredient for attaining success, or coming back
from adversity. I remember watching the great golfer Gary Player
being interviewed some time ago, and he made the statement: "It just
seems that the harder I work, the luckier I get." For some reason,

maybe obvious, maybe not, this is very much the truth in my case also. It seems that when I do the best, I am working the hardest.

Toward the end of the 1980s and the beginning of the 1990s, I was truly not working at the pace I had worked at before. I wasn't focused and really thought that life and success just came hand in hand. I thought I was just better than the rest. When I began to relax and take it easier, things began to fall apart. Yes, I know, the economy went south during this period, but I am convinced that if I had maintained the same work ethic I had during the 1970s and most of the 1980s, there would have been no recession for me. Obviously, you've got to be blessed with certain God-given talents or traits, but no matter what you are lucky enough to have, working hard is often the common denominator for success.

I know many people who are blessed with unusually great abilities who consistently lose out and, in fact, get beaten up by people without their talent who just work them to death. Now, if you work hard and also happen to have the ability, there's no stopping you. Many people have the talent but have never worked hard enough to let it show through. Don't be lazy, don't lose focus; just go out and get it done.

Another element of success, which I hate to mention here because it truly can't be acquired, is luck. You can be born lucky. Maybe your parents are smart and you inherited great intelligence. Perhaps you're born into wealth, and you have access to the best schools and privileges. (I think the ultimate gift would be to be born happy.) I remember once speaking to a friend who is very successful. He sat down next to me and flew into a rage when I explained my theory of luck. He simply stated, "Donald, there is no such thing as luck. You make your own luck." I was amazed. Here was a guy who was born to a prominent family—a family of some wealth, but great genes—and he got the genes in spades.

What you *can* do, however, is help coax luck into your life by working hard. I have many examples, in my own life, of being at meetings or places where I did not have to be. Most of these I felt obligated to attend, but it was usually at such a meeting that I would meet someone who was ultimately able to help me out later or to help me create a success in some form. If I was not at the meeting, I would not have met that person, and that success would most likely not have happened. By being there, even against my own best wishes, I got things accomplished.

Once I was having a problem with a certain politician who was fighting me very hard on a particular development. Somehow, and I still don't know exactly why, a friend of mine called and invited me to a surprise party he was giving for this politician. I was in Florida, and the party was in New York. The last thing I wanted to do was get on a plane and travel for hours in order to go to a party for a man I couldn't stand in the first place. But I felt energetic enough and decided that it would be in my best interests.

By the time I arrived, however, it was already very late and the party was starting to break up. I saw the politician about to leave, but he was really impressed that I would journey from Florida to be with him. He really appreciated it, so we sat down and talked. By the end of the evening, he turned out to be my "new best friend," and everything went very smoothly between us from then on. He was actually a very good guy and a positive force—but I would not have known this if I had decided to stay in Florida and watch the sun, the moon, and the stars.

I have noticed over the years that those who are guarded or, to put it somewhat more coldly, slightly paranoid, end up being the most successful. How often do you read about heirs of the wealthy who are open and easy prey to the slicksters, sharks, and others who feed on the weak?

People who inherit fortunes are very interesting to me. I see it down in Palm Beach all the time. But I respect those who realize their limitations and don't want to take chances. They got lucky. I call them members of the lucky-sperm club—they inherited wealth. I've noticed that the lucky ones are usually very cheap. They never pick up the tab, live very frugally, and are seldom the life of the party. They know that if they lose their money, they don't have the ability to make it back. The more unlucky ones are those who inherit wealth and decide that they are going to be the next great success, but they don't have the talent. Their money goes fast. It's not a pretty picture. I have seen it often, and seldom is there a sadder scene than a family that starts out with wealth and ends up fighting just to survive.

I know one family, from Bedford, a wealthy town in Westchester County, New York, that was seemingly blessed with everything. The father was extremely successful on Wall Street, and the kids, outwardly at least, really seemed to have it all—they were handsome and articulate, and you just would never have bet against them. But after the father died, leaving his entire fortune to the children, things started going very wrong. Within five years the business had totally collapsed and the beautiful Bedford house and New York City apartment were taken back by the banks.

The last time I saw one of the sons, the leader of the pack, he was working in a grocery store, barely able to survive. I could see he was a broken man. It was very sad. It's very hard to start at such a high level and go down so low. I don't think that reading *The Art of the Comeback* would help him much, because the fall was so severe and his pride has been so badly damaged. Thinking back to the glory days of Bedford, it must be very hard for him, in all fairness, just to get out of bed in the morning and go to work. In order to come back, you need confidence—and his confidence must be totally blown by the fact that he lost so much so fast. It's hard to think of yourself as a winner when you go through the family fortune in a few years and never sample even a morsel of success. But you never know, maybe he, too, can come back. Hence: Be suspect, be *guarded.* Let some paranoia reign! You've got to realize that you have something other people want. Don't let them take it away.

Passion is another key ingredient to success and perhaps even more so to coming back. If you don't have passion about who you are, about what you are trying to be, about where you are going, you might as well close this book right now and give up. Go get a job and just relax because you have no chance of making it. Passion is the essence of life and certainly the essence of success. If you work hard without passion, you're just wasting lots of energy. You really have to want to do something important.

Dr. Norman Vincent Peale, the great pastor of the Marble Collegiate Church and the author of one of the best-selling books of all time, *The Power of Positive Thinking,* referred to passion as enthusiasm. Norman Vincent Peale was an amazing man. I only got to watch him toward the end of his life, but he was truly inspiring. He took a very old and beautiful church on lower Fifth Avenue and made it into a hotbed of religion. On Sunday mornings, when other churches sat empty, you couldn't even get near Marble Collegiate. When Dr. Peale was preaching, the church had two sessions, which sat throngs of people. It wasn't enough. They had to open up offices and rooms all over the church and wire them up with closed-circuit television sets. Dr. Peale commanded the pulpit like no one else. He was perhaps the greatest speaker I have ever watched.

The enthusiasm and passion he had for his work was totally infectious. You would leave church and say, "Gee whiz, it's too bad that's over, I would love to hear some more." When Dr. Peale wrote *The Power of Positive Thinking,* he meant just that, think positively. But what he also was saying was that this is not a false way of thinking.

Thinking positively has to be a natural thing. You don't just say to yourself, "I'm going to do it, I'm going to do it." You never let the negative thoughts even enter your mind.

It is imperative that you do something you really love. Vince Lombardi, the great football coach, was famous for saying, "You've got to love it." He believed you would not be a winner on the football field if you didn't love tackling or hitting really hard. The same thing is true in life and business: You've got to tackle and hit real hard. I know many people who have ability but are just doing things they don't want to be doing. Their enthusiasm runs low, and they don't work as hard as they should. It's because, as Lombardi always said, "they don't love it."

I think of a man I know whose life has never gotten going. He grew up rich and was very spoiled, and he never had real incentive to accomplish much. One day recently I received a call from him because I am building two great golf courses in Westchester County, and he wanted to give me a reference on a contractor who had just done a great job for him. He had been a member of a country club, also in Westchester, for many years, and now they were redoing the greens and much of the landscaping, and he was heading the committee that was responsible for this project. I was surprised at how enthusiastic he sounded about the endeavor. He told me how he would arrive at six or seven o'clock almost every morning to inspect the work. Nothing could be done without his approval; every blade of grass had to be perfect.

What was interesting to me, however, was the confidence and enthusiasm that this gentleman expressed. I had known him for a long time, and I had never heard it before. When I asked him about the rest of his life, he virtually didn't want to waste the time to tell me about it. He kept steering the conversation back to the golf course and how much fun he was having. After listening to him for ten minutes, I said that he should go into that business. He almost didn't know what I meant, but I was very insistent. "Look," I told him, "you've never really been very successful, and yet you're a smart guy. You never liked what you did, and that was always obvious to me and everybody around you. This is the first time I've ever had a conversation with you where you are upbeat, enthusiastic, and smart as hell on the topic. Get out of what you're doing and go into golf-course design and construction. Even if you don't make as much money, you'll enjoy your life, and I predict you'll really be successful at it. Don't even think about it for a minute."

He didn't take my advice. I saw him recently, and he had faded back into his former somber mood. I asked him how things were going, and he said, in a barely audible voice, "Okay." I asked him how he did with the golf course, and he explained that the project was finished about a year ago and there was nothing left for him to do. It had come out beautifully, and now a new committee had taken over. Basically, he didn't have the courage to make the move even though it would have been best for him. I'm still working on him, and I'll probably succeed. And when I am successful, he will be successful.

The courage to make a switch, even if it seems like a ridiculous one, is also an ingredient of success. There are times when a change in life's course does seem strange, but it may well be necessary in order to create success. And success can't be measured just in dollars and cents; it has to be measured in happiness, too. I know many rich people who are extremely unhappy and really should be doing something else.

Going against the tide is often a very clever thing to do. While it can involve unbelievable risks, and while I cannot say that it's a primary factor for success, often going in the opposite direction can lead to the highest level of achievement. When I decided to keep 40 Wall Street as an office building, I was very much going against the tide. Everyone in lower Manhattan was converting their buildings to apartments—and with good reason. The apartment market is hot as a pistol, and lower Manhattan is fast becoming a fantastic residential community. But I had a building that was well located for business and much less costly to convert into offices than apartments. It was also a spectacular structure. I decided that rather than going the safe route, the route that everybody else was taking, I would head in the exact opposite direction. It turns out that many, many buildings are under construction now as apartments, and they will all do fine, but I have the only major office building in downtown Manhattan that is in peak condition and a prime location. I am signing up tenants as fast as the leases can be drawn and at rents that are far higher than anything I ever expected.

Good management is a key to success and always will be. The ability to manage is a unique trait, but often good managers, by themselves, do not have the many other ingredients needed to truly succeed. One who does is a man named Pat Foley. During the early eighties, Pat was the president of the Hyatt Hotel Corporation and took Hyatt to a position of prominence in the hotel industry. Under his leadership it was a dynamic company, well managed at every level, and a company with great promotional and architectural sense. Pat really helped put Hyatt on the map.

I'll never forget my first major experience with Pat. I had just finished construction of the Grand Hyatt Hotel on Forty-second Street and Park Avenue, and the hotel was getting ready to open. I was very proud of my achievements because, at a very young age, I had brought the hotel in significantly ahead of schedule and under budget. It was now Hyatt's turn to show its stuff and manage this beautiful project I had created.

During the late seventies and early eighties, I was extremely busy on many fronts, building the foundations of what was to become the Trump Organization. I didn't really have the time or patience to attend management meetings at the Hyatt Hotel, as important as those meetings were. Instead, I asked Ivana to attend. The problem was that the general manager of the hotel, a fantastic guy in all other respects, had a hard time taking orders from women. When Ivana would say something, he wouldn't listen. When Ivana would ask questions, he would barely even answer them. He had absolutely no respect for Ivana, and it wasn't Ivana's fault. He was a strong guy and a good manager, but when it came to women, he wasn't open to their ideas. Perhaps he was one who thought, incorrectly, that a woman's place is in the kitchen.

In any event, a problem was arising, and arising fast. Ivana would come home and cry that they weren't giving her the respect she deserved at the Grand Hyatt. I called the manager, and while he was very nice, he really wasn't open to letting her get involved. Then I called Pat Foley, the manager's boss, and explained the problem. He said to me, "Look, Donald, I disagree with you, but if you want Ivana involved, then I'm going to get her involved." He called a meeting of the manager, Ivana, me, and himself. We sat around a table having breakfast at the hotel's Crystal Fountain restaurant. He told his manager, in the strongest of tones, that he wanted Ivana's total involvement. He wanted her every word to be appreciated. Whenever anything was bought, sold, moved, or changed, he wanted the manager to call her and get her permission. He made Ivana feel truly important and good about herself.

Over the next number of months, Ivana was called incessantly by the manager and everybody else in the Hyatt about everything from buying a sheet or how to clean the pots and pans to the cost of detergent. Ivana got so bored and tired she didn't want to hear it anymore, but she was happy that she was being treated with respect. What Pat Foley did was keep his partner, me, happy. Rather than saying no to her involvement, he said what the hell, she's going to get tired of it soon anyway and we'll never hear from her again.

Pat left Hyatt a very strong and dynamic company and went to DHL, where he did the same thing. He built it into a dynamic force, and it is now, starting from a small base, one of the most respected companies in its field. Pat is one of the people you read about who truly manages through personality. When he was running the Hyatt Hotel chain, he would walk into kitchens, grab chefs he had never even seen before, give them hugs and tell them what a great job they were doing. When he left, the entire kitchen was upbeat, and in a time when chefs were almost impossible to get, there was no way they were going to be leaving Hyatt.

It is very important to be respected if you are going to be successful—especially in your own mind. People have to respect you for who you are and what you've done; the only way they are going to do so is if you earn that respect. Despite that, people will often want to take advantage of you in any way they can. You've got to let them know who's the boss, and you can't take any crap. People rule in many ways. But whether through fear or respect, your opponents and even your friends must know they can't push you around. If they can, you're not the boss. They are. They also have to know that if they do try to take advantage of you, there is a price for them to pay. Be firm, be strong, and be fair, but if someone tries to screw you, screw them back harder than they ever got screwed before.

Above all, keep your eye on the shop. I said it before, and I'll say it again: If I'd kept my eye on the ball, I might have been able to anticipate the systemic economic problems in the early nineties. But I didn't. I left the day-to-day business up to others. Apparently my friend Meshulum Riklis did the same.

Riklis is a hardened dealmaker, who, unfortunately for him, is perhaps more famous for having been married to Pia Zadora than for having made $1 billion two or three times. He came into my office at one point and told me how he had made a great deal of money, then gone out, hired executives to run his company, found a new and beautiful wife, and relaxed. He then related how much of that fortune was lost by the executives while he sat back and enjoyed the good life. "I had to go immediately back to work again, Donald," he said, and he rebuilt his fortune. This happened a second time to Ric, and frankly, it looks to me like it's happening a third. As he left the office he told me, "You know, Donald, I've gone through this twice before, but now that I'm seventy-five it's different." Pia, who he worked so hard to make into a star despite her obvious shortcomings, had left him and later married a much younger man. I couldn't help feeling a little sorry for him.

In order to be truly successful, you need a great deal of drive and stamina. Seldom can success be achieved without an almost complete and universal focus on what it is you're trying to accomplish. Sure, on occasion someone might have an idea so brilliant that others are able to take it and make a lot of money for that someone—that is, if he is able to protect himself legally in the first place.

Just as you can't be successful without focus, you cannot do anything if you are unable to deal with stress. One thing I know for sure: When the going gets tough, don't reach for a drink. I've seen alcohol ruin the lives of chief executives. I've seen it destroy marriages and rip apart families. I've seen it kill. My older brother, Fred junior, whom I loved dearly, died of alcoholism.

When I open the newspaper and read of the assult on the tobacco companies, I often ask myself why alcohol companies aren't under a similar attack. Far more people have been killed by alcoholism and its related problems than have ever been killed by cigarettes. Let's wake up, lawyers!

In concluding a list of important points for success and/or comeback, the one I am most proud to have learned is to never take success for granted. I would have never had my glitch in the early 1990s had I realized this at the time. Success is not easy. It is hard-won, with many elements going into it. I realize that now. Don't take success for granted, and you'll never have to worry about it again.

As I close this book, I'm going into perhaps the most exciting part of my life. I am starting 610 Park Avenue, at Sixty-fifth Street and

Park, with Colony Capital and its head, Tom Barrack, one of the smartest people in business. 610 Park will be a superluxury apartment development in perhaps the best location in New York City. It will use the skeleton and exterior walls of the Mayfair Regent Hotel. When completed, it will be one of the most luxurious and beautiful buildings in New York. In a similar vein, I am also converting 100 Central Park South, an eighty-three-unit apartment house that faces the park.

I am also working with the great Korean company Daewoo, on a superluxury high-rise tower directly across from the UN secretariat on United Nations Plaza. When complete, this tower, to be called the Trump World Tower, will be eighty stories tall and have views of the United Nations and beyond unsurpassed anywhere in the city. It will also have a hotel section and restaurant, much like Trump International Hotel and Tower at 1 Central Park West. Trump World Tower will be the tallest residential building in the country.

By the time this book is complete, the West Side Railroad Yards will be in full bloom. Two major towers are already started, and an additional two or three will begin shortly. As stated before, this is the largest development project ever approved by the New York City Planning Commission, and it will be built, depending on the market, over a period of seven to ten years. The end result will be 5,700 units of housing overlooking the Hudson River, behind Lincoln Center, stretching from Fifty-ninth Street to Seventy-second. This will truly be a great city within the greatest city of them all, New York.

Mar-a-Lago has become such a great success as a club that I've embarked on a number of other club projects that are very exciting. I'm building the Trump National Golf Club in Briarcliff Manor, a wonderful community in Westchester County. When completed, about a year from now, this club will be one of the best in New York. I am in the middle of zoning the Seven Springs development in Bedford, New York's wealthiest community, a 214-acre parcel of land surrounded by hundreds of acres of national wildlife preserve, only a short distance outside the city. This is probably the best land I have ever seen for a high-end golf course. When completed, the Trump Mansion at Seven Springs will be one of the greatest golf courses anywhere in the world. The third course I am building has already been started, directly opposite the main entrance to the private jetport at the Palm Beach International Airport. This will be called Trump International Golf Club, and I hope to make it the finest in Florida.

The Rockefeller mansion at Seven Springs, soon to be a plush Trump golf club. Get in early. Memberships are now selling for $250,000.

Many people have already joined, and the club hasn't even opened. At Trump International, we will be moving close to three million yards of earth, almost a record for a golf course. The end result will be breathtaking.

With FAI Insurance, I will be revisiting the St. Moritz Hotel. When I sold the St. Moritz to Alan Bond in the late eighties for $180 million, he had to borrow the money from the Australian insurance company. In the end, FAI foreclosed on Alan and took over the property. I am now in a joint venture with FAI, which is headed by Rodney Adler, a brilliant young entrepreneur from Australia who took over the company after his father's death. Most institutional people would have sold the St. Moritz in the terrible down market of the early nineties, and they would have lost a fortune. Because he did not let this happen, because he had the courage to hold on and weather the bad storm, Rodney, in my opinion, is going to make a great deal of money for his shareholders. We are converting the St. Moritz into a superluxury condominium tower that will be among the most beautiful anywhere. I am very proud of this project. I was very lucky with it the first time, in that I made a great deal of money in so little time. It is always nice to revisit early successes.

My casino company continues to thrive, but the public marketplace has not embraced it the way I feel it should. In the end, I believe my stockholders will be very happy with what we are doing. Just like Trump bondholders before them, who had a difficult spell during the early nineties and now are extremely happy they held, I believe that the Trump Hotels & Casino Resorts stock will be one of the really good ones over the next number of years.

I'll be working with my partners from CDL, headed by Kwek Leng Beng, the brilliant Singaporean who this year received an award as the most outstanding businessman in Asia, and Prince Awaleed, who has already become a legendary businessman for some of the great deals he has made over the last seven years, including Citibank and EuroDisney. We will be converting a number of underutilized floors at the Plaza Hotel into superluxury condominiums.

This will most likely be the last book I write. To do it right takes a lot of time and patience. More important, the things I am stressing, whether they be for success or coming back, really are not going to change. Working hard and working smart, whether in the 1980s, 1990s, or in the year 2000, will always be the ticket. I have really enjoyed writing this book, even more than the other two. I am at a very happy time in my life. I have seen my company through a storm—a storm of great proportions that has devastated many companies and people—and I am now bigger and stronger than ever before. I have learned a lot, and I have spelled much of it out in the pages of this book. I just hope that people are able to take some of my words and apply them to their own lives, especially if they are troubled, looking to succeed or, very simply, to get back what they once had—and more. There could be no greater joy for me than to hear from people that this book made a big difference in their lives. If you want to tell me about your comeback, send me a letter. You know the address. Meanwhile, work hard and don't allow yourself to understand the meaning of the word *defeat*. Above all, enjoy what you're doing, and the only thing you'll have is victory, victory, victory!

ACKNOWLEDGMENTS

I could not have done what I did to come back without certain people who stuck by me every step of the way.

Nick Ribis, my trusted chief executive officer, is a good friend and a truly outstanding businessman who has completely helped me to turn around my casino interests in Atlantic City and more.

My executive assistant, Norma Foerderer, is someone I will never be able to thank enough. The title executive assistant does not even begin to describe what she does for me and for The Trump Organization.

I would also like to take the opportunity to thank my former chief financial officer, Stephen Bollenbach. Steve was a tremendous help to me. He's smart, efficient, and not afraid to speak his mind. Steve is now working with Barron Hilton, the brilliant and farsighted chairman of Hilton Hotels, and I have no doubt that he will do an outstanding job as he has already done.

There are many others who have stood by me and helped me along the way, including Abe Wallach, my head of real estate; Bernie Diamond, my chief counsel; Dino Bradlee; Allen Weisselberg; David Malitzky; Andy Weiss; Charlie Reiss. I would also like to thank my three loyal secretaries, Rhona Graff, Anita Sharpe, and Rachel Ryan, for putting up with the madness. You've been great.

At Random House and Times Books, I am particularly grateful to Harold Evans, Times Books publisher Peter Bernstein, associate publisher Carie Freimuth, publicity director Mary Beth Roche, and my editor Jonathan Karp.

Another crucial participant in my comeback is "Big" Matt Calamari, my chief of security. Matt does everything and anything necessary to make my life safe and as easy as possible, and he does it with iron style. Matt always tells me that if he was not six feet, four inches and 265 pounds of pure muscle, people would think he's smart. Kind of like the dumb-blonde stereotype. I couldn't have come back without him because if he hadn't been around, I might not have been here to come back at all.

—D. T.

I would like to thank my unwavering and loyal assistant Heather Parks—we shared quite a few bleary all-nighters. I also wish to thank Dino Bradlee, Candace Bushnell, Josh Levine, Alan Marcus, and Fidel Marquez for their stalwart support and unflagging good looks. Of course, Binky Urban, whose indispensable guidance sustained me, and Jonathan Karp, my editor, who is just a love. Most of all, The Donald: he believed when others didn't, and never stopped believing.

—K. B.

INDEX

KATE BOHNER began her career in the mergers and acquisitions department at Lazard Frères after studying business and international studies at the University of Pennsylvania. She later moved to London to work in recapitalizations and restructurings. She left Lazard for Columbia University, where she studied journalism and writing on a Reader's Digest Literary Foundation Fellowship. Upon graduating, Ms. Bohner joined *Forbes* as a fact checker, and was promoted to writer, editor, and columnist soon thereafter. She's currently an on-camera correspondent for CNBC.